8993

B E  Y A M E N

Library
Oakland S.U.M.

BEFORE YOU SAY "AMEN"

VICTOR BOOKS®
A DIVISION OF SCRIPTURE PRESS PUBLICATIONS INC.
USA CANADA ENGLAND

Most Scripture quotations are taken from the *Holy Bible, New International Version*, © 1973, 1978, 1984, International Bible Society. Used by permission of Zondervan Bible Publishers. Other quotations are from the *New American Standard Bible* (NASB), © the Lockman Foundation 1960, 1962, 1963, 1968, 1971, 1972, 1973, 1975, 1977; and from J.B. Phillips: *The New Testament in Modern English*, Revised Edition, © J.B. Phillips, 1958, 1960, 1972, permission of Macmillan Publishing Co. and Collins Publishers.

Recommended Dewey Decimal Classification: 242
Suggested Subject Heading: PRAYER

Library of Congress Catalog Card Number: 88-62862
ISBN: 0-89639-637-6

© 1989 by SP Publications, Inc. All rights reserved. Printed in the United States of America. No part of this book may be reproduced without written permission, except for brief quotations in books, critical articles, and reviews.

VICTOR BOOKS
A division of SP Publications, Inc.
        Wheaton, Illinois 60187

•CONTENTS•

Recognition to Beth Donigan Seversen
for assistance
in researching and formulating
parts of this book.

• INTRODUCTION •

A mother was preparing for dinner guests one evening, so she reminded her little girl to say her prayers before she went to bed.

Next morning, the mother asked, "Did you say your prayers last night?"

"Well," the little one explained, "I got down on my knees and started to say them, and all of a sudden I thought: I bet God gets awfully tired of hearing the same old prayer over and over.

"So I crawled into bed and told Him the story of the three bears."

I don't recommend that you start telling God fairy tales, but I agree with the little girl! God must get pretty tired of hearing the same old prayers over and over again from some of us. Maybe we should begin to "say something" relevant to our Heavenly Father.

• BEFORE YOU BEGIN •

People who gather together for Bible study are likely to be at different places in their spiritual lives, and their study materials should be flexible enough to meet their different needs. This book is designed to be used as a Bible study guide for such groups in homes or churches. It can also be used by individuals who are studying on their own. The lessons are written in five distinct sections, so that they can be used in a variety of situations. Groups and individuals alike can choose to use the elements they find most useful in the order they find most beneficial.

These studies will help you learn some new truths from the Bible as well as how to dig out those truths. You will learn not only *what* the Bible says, but how to use Scripture to deepen your relationship with Jesus Christ by obeying it and applying it in daily living. These studies will also provide an opportunity for potential leaders to learn how to lead a discussion in a nonthreatening setting.

What You'll Need
For each study you will need a Bible and this Bible study guide. You might also want to have a notebook in which to record your thoughts and discoveries from your personal study and group meetings. A notebook could also be used to record prayer requests from the group.

The Sections
Food for Thought. This is a devotional narrative that introduces the topic, person, or passage featured in the lesson. There are several ways it can be used. Each person could read it before coming to the group meeting, and someone could briefly summarize it at the beginning. It could be read silently by each person at the beginning of the session, or it could be read aloud, by one or several group members. (Suggested time: 10 minutes)

Talking It Over. This section contains discussion questions to help you review what you learned in Food for Thought. There are also questions to help you apply the narrative's truths to daily life. The person who leads the discussion of these questions need not be a trained or experienced teacher. All that is needed is someone to keep things moving and facilitate group interaction. (Suggested time: 30 minutes)

Praying It Through. This is a list of suggestions for prayer based on the lesson. You may want to use all the suggestions or eliminate some in order to leave more time for personal sharing and prayer requests. (Suggested time: 20 minutes)

Digging Deeper. The questions in this section are also related to the passage, topic, or character from the lesson. But they will not always be limited to the exact passage or character from Food for Thought. Passages and characters from both the Old and New Testaments will appear in this section, in order to show how God has worked through *all* of history in people's lives. These questions will require a little more thinking and some digging into Scripture, as well as some use of Bible study tools. Participants will be stretched as they become experienced in the "how-tos" of Bible study. (Suggested time: 45 minutes)

Tool Chest. The Tool Chest contains a description of a specific type of Bible study help and includes an explanation of how it is used. An example of the tool is given, and an example of it or excerpt from it is usually included in the Digging Deeper study.

The Bible study helps in the Tool Chest can be purchased by anyone who desires to build a basic library of Bible study reference books and other tools. They would also be good additions to a church library. Some are reasonably inexpensive, but others are quite expensive. A few may be available in your local library or in a seminary or college library. A group might decide to purchase one tool during each series and build a corporate tool chest for all the members of the group to use. You can never be too young a Christian to begin to master Bible study helps, nor can you be too old to learn new methods of rightly dividing the Word of truth.

Options for Group Use
Different groups, made up of people at diverse stages of spiritual growth, will want to use the elements in this book in different ways. Here are a few suggestions to get you started, but be creative and sensitive to your group's needs.

☐ Spend 5-15 minutes at the beginning of the group time introducing yourselves and having group members answer an icebreaker question. (Sample icebreaker questions are included under Tips for Leaders.)

☐ Extend the prayer time to include sharing of prayer requests, praise items, or things group members have learned recently in their times of personal Bible study.

☐ The leader could choose questions for discussion from the Digging Deeper section based on whether participants have prepared ahead of time or not.

☐ The entire group could break into smaller groups to allow different groups to use different sections. (The smaller groups could move to other rooms in the home or church where you are meeting.)

Tips for Leaders
Preparation
1. Pray for the Holy Spirit's guidance as you study, that you will be equipped to teach the lesson and make it appealing and applicable.

2. Read through the entire lesson and any Bible passages or verses that are mentioned. Answer all the questions.

3. Become familiar enough with the lesson that, if time in the group is running out, you know which questions could most easily be left out.

4. Gather all the items you will need for the study: name tags, extra pens, extra Bibles.

The Meeting

1. Start and end on time.

2. Have everyone wear a name tag until group members know one another's names.

3. Have each person introduce himself or herself, or ask regular attenders to introduce guests.

4. For each meeting, pick an icebreaker question or another activity to help group members get to know one another better.

5. Use any good ideas to make everyone feel comfortable.

The Discussion

1. Ask the questions, but try to let the group answer. Don't be afraid of silence. Reword the question if it is unclear to the group or answer it yourself to clarify.

2. Encourage everyone to participate. If someone is shy, ask that person to answer an opinion question or another nonthreatening question. If someone tends to monopolize the discussion, thank that person for his or her contribution and ask if someone else has anything he or she would like to add. (Or ask that person to make the coffee!)

3. If someone gives an incorrect answer, don't bluntly or tactlessly tell him or her so. If it is partly right, reinforce that. Ask if anyone else has any thoughts on the subject. (Disagree agreeably!)

4. Avoid tangents. If someone is getting off the subject, ask that person how his or her point relates to the lesson.

5. Don't feel threatened if someone asks a question you can't answer. Tell the person you don't know but will find out before the next meeting—then be sure to find out! Or ask if someone would like to research and present the answer at the group's next meeting.

Icebreaker Questions

The purpose of these icebreaker questions is to help the people in your group get to know one another over the course of the study. The questions you use when your group members don't know one another very well should be very general and nonthreatening. As time goes on, your questions can become more focused and specific. Always give group members the option of passing if they think a question is too personal.

What do you like to do for fun?

What is your favorite season? dessert? book?

What would be your ideal vacation?

What exciting thing happened to you this week?

What was the most memorable thing you did with your family when you were a child?

What one word best describes the way you feel today?

Tell three things you are thankful for.

Imagine that your house is on fire. What three things would you try to take with you on your way out?

If you were granted one wish, what would it be?

What experience of your past would you most enjoy reliving?

What quality do you most appreciate in a friend?

What is your pet peeve?

What is something you are learning to do or trying to get better at?

What is your greatest hope?

What is your greatest fear?

What one thing would you like to change about yourself?

What has been the greatest accomplishment of your life?

What has been the greatest disappointment of your life?

Need More Help?

Here is a list of books that contain helpful information on leading discussions and working in groups:

> *How to Lead Small Group Bible Studies* (NavPress, 1982).
> *Creative Bible Learning for Adults*, Monroe Marlowe and Bobbie Reed (Regal, 1977).
> *Getting Together*, Em Griffin (InterVarsity Press, 1982).
> *Good Things Come in Small Groups* (InterVarsity Press, 1985).

One Last Thought

This book is a tool you can use whether you have one or one hundred people who want to study the Bible and whether you have one or no teachers. Don't wait for a brilliant Bible study leader to appear—most such teachers acquired their skills by starting with a book like this and learning as they went along. Torrey said, "The best way to begin, is to begin." Happy beginnings!

1
Where Do I Begin?

•FOOD FOR THOUGHT•

Prayer is conversation with God. He speaks to us through His Word; we speak to Him through our words.

God listens to man's side of the conversation. He hears people who don't belong to Him. I know this because He heard my prayer when I didn't belong to Him, before I was a Christian. I became a believer by praying a simple prayer asking God to accept me and come into my life. Because I know God heard my prayer, I can encourage others who don't know Him to pray. People like Cornelius. People who have been praying to God all their lives and yet have never personally met the One to whom they pray. Because of what happened to Cornelius, we need to tell others that God will hear their prayers.

Maybe you have always "said your prayers," but like Cornelius have never been personally presented with an available relationship with the One at whom you have aimed those petitions! "Heaven on earth" begins to happen in your life when you are personally introduced to the Lord God who wants to walk and talk with you—in fact, live within you, by the Holy Spirit. Would you like to accept Him just as Cornelius did? Then let me help you in case you do not know what to say.

As a student at Homerton College, Cambridge, I wanted to accept Jesus Christ and His Holy Spirit into my life. I knew I was a sinner and needed forgiveness. A girl asked me if I would like to begin this relationship with Deity, and I told her I wanted to very much! But I didn't know how to start *my* side of the conversation. I didn't know what to say. I was feeling clumsy, awkward, and even a little stupid, so my friend offered to share a prayer that I could make my own. Here it is. You may use it too.

"Dear God, I know Jesus lived a sinless life and died on the cross that my sins may be forgiven. I know I need to thank Him and ask Him to personally forgive me and accept me, even as I now accept His Holy Spirit into my life. Come into my heart, Lord, and begin to talk to me from within. Then, Lord, teach me to pray. Amen."

I'm sure Cornelius' prayers became quite different after his relationship with God was established that day. He began to learn, as we begin to learn, that any relationship without communication between the participants starves to death. What greater misery can be imagined than marriage partners who never speak to each other, children and parents who avoid conversation, or people who are supposed to be friends sitting in silence, wondering what on earth to talk about. Relationship depends largely on verbal communication; and in man's relationship with God, prayer is the verbal communication.

John the Baptist was one of God's greatest VIPs. Jesus said so: "Of man born of woman—there is no greater!"

What were the characteristics of one of God's VIPs? There were many: courage, humility, a certainty about what he was supposed to be achieving; but one of the most important characteristics was that of a "desert" lifestyle. We read in Luke 1:80, "[John] lived in the desert until he appeared publicly to Israel."

There are other examples of the desert lifestyle in the pages of Scripture. And there are also illustrations of those without it! There is Martha in Luke 10—irritated with her sister, with her Lord and, I am sure, with herself for being irritated! She was always too busy to go to the "desert" and spend time with God.

Saul, having met Jesus on the Damascus Road, became an absolute menace to the church. True, he was busy preaching and teaching, but observe the reaction to his ministry. He reminds me of a hot potato straight out of the fire! No one wanted to hold onto him for long. He was thrown from one lot of unbelieving believers to the next. They didn't dare believe he was for real. He took off on one of the speediest and most disastrous evangelistic campaigns on record. From Damascus to Jerusalem to Antioch and finally, to the churches' great relief, into the deserts of Arabia. Then and only then did the churches "rest"! (Acts 9:31)

Is there a Saul or two in your church? Oh, they may have a

dramatic testimony, a glory story, and be loaded with talent and spiritual gifts, but the church is constantly in turmoil because of them. The answer is quite simple—they need a desert lifestyle. When Saul came out of the Arabian wilderness years later, he came back to the same church with the Book of Romans in his heart and a new attitude. Then, and only then, he brought an edifying word instead of a divisive one. Then he began church planting instead of church leveling; and, incidentally, he was given a new name—he became the Apostle Paul!

The Lord goes to extraordinary pains to get us alone. He will move heaven and earth to provide us a desert. He will ask us, beckon us, cajole us, command us, persuade us, or chase us there. He may even use the "desert" of a hospital bed where there is only one way to look—up! I don't know what it will take for you, but I do know that our greatest transactions take place *alone,* and you can't be a VIP without that desert lifestyle.

But you may ask, what do I do when I get to the desert? You *talk!* Now, a conversation with anyone is going to take time. Conversations are not usually dependent on age, clever words or lack of them, or even similar cultural backgrounds. Any two people can communicate if both are willing to do so. But it does take a decision to spend time together. The more time given to that, the better the relationship can become; and the better the relationship can become, the better communication should be!

No one has any more time than you have. It is the discipline and stewardship of your time that is important. The management of time is the management of self; therefore, if you manage time with God, He will begin to manage you.

Colossians 4:5 says, "Make the best possible use of your time" (PH). Psalm 31:15 says, "My times are in your hands." This doesn't happen automatically. You have to put your time into those hands. It's not a question of whenever you can squeeze some time with God into your weekly schedule. It is a question of giving your weekly schedule to Him and letting *Him* squeeze other things out so that you two can begin to meet together.

The great example we have before us is the example of our Lord Jesus Christ. To begin with, He stepped from the dimension of eternity into time, that He might achieve in time eternal accomplishments. That is what time is for—to achieve those things for which the minutes, days, and hours are lent to us. At the age of 12, Jesus said, "I must be about My Father's business." So must we, and there is no way we can do that unless time is spent asking the

Father which part of His business we must see to each day.

There are a number of examples in the Old Testament of busy men who made their time with God the number-one priority in their lives. The example of Daniel is perhaps the best pattern for us.

I would honestly have to say that my "quiet time" is not worth a den of lions! Is yours? I would like mine to be!

Perhaps some of you have decided you have such irregular life-styles that it is impossible to make a regular habit or discipline of a "desert" rendezvous with God. There is always the unexpected, the emergency, the interruption. But according to Daniel it is in the unexpected situation that you *react to certain habits formed in secret!*

I am sure Nehemiah had a "Daniel" habit, and it was this daily practice of being in touch with God that enabled him to link up with the wisdom he sought in a very dangerous situation.

In conclusion, we can say we need to be like Daniel and Nehemiah every day. We need to be constantly referring to God throughout our daily experiences. Our attitude of dependence will stem from our habit of daily devotions. Take your calendar each Monday morning and block off ten minutes every day of the week. As your schedule differs, so will the time you put aside for Him. So make an appointment on your calendar and then keep it! Be as conscientious about that as you are about your club or tennis dates. Start now and become a Daniel.

Then practice talking to God on an informal basis this week. Chat with Him. Just talk in your mind all day long about everything. He is "within" you, so you two can be having a great conversation. Use emergency prayers when needed. They are simple to learn. Here is one I use all the time: "Help!" Try it; He will help you, for He is your Counselor and Friend and is within you to help all that needs helping (and if you are like me, that means He's going to be very busy!).

•TALKING IT OVER•

1. READ AND DISCUSS TOGETHER.   *6 minutes*

Turn in your Bible to Acts 10:1-4, and read around the group. Write down the answers to the following questions and discuss the information you have gathered.

☐ What do you learn about Cornelius' prayer life from verse 2?

☐ What do you think God thought about this uncircumcised Roman soldier's prayers? (vv. 4, 31)

☐ How did God go about answering those petitions? What does this teach you about God's attitude toward a "real" seeker's prayer, whoever is praying it? (vv. 3, 9-19, 34-35, 44-48)

2. LIST AND PRIORITIZE.   *8 minutes*

Priorities determine your daily, weekly, and monthly schedule. Make a list of five of your responsibilities for today and five of the things you plan to do for yourself. Mark them honestly in order of priority, 1–10. There are 24 hours in a day; 168 hours in a week. If there are 56 hours to sleep, that leaves 112 waking hours. Distribute honestly the portion of time you give to the following per week: husband/wife or parents, children or family, work, leisure, personal time with God, God's service.

☐ If you are working on your own, stop right now and ask yourself, "Is God getting a good deal?" Pray about that now.

☐ If you are working in a group, discuss your conclusions for a few moments.

3. READ AND ANSWER QUESTIONS.   *11 minutes*

Turn to Daniel 6:4-15. Read it through; then answer the following questions:

☐ Describe Daniel's prayer life (v. 10).

☐ How do you know Daniel's prayer life was important to him?

17

☐ Is my time with God that important?

Read Nehemiah 2:1-6; then answer these questions:
☐ What national problem did Nehemiah become aware of?
☐ What was his response?
☐ Why did he have to answer immediately?
☐ How would you describe this sort of praying?

4. PRAY.   *5 minutes*

Now it is time to talk to God about these things we have been learning. Spend five minutes either in quiet personal prayer or in conversational prayer around the group. Pray about what God has taught you from the lives of Daniel and Nehemiah.

•PRAYING IT THROUGH•

Suggested Times

1. (On your own) Are you sure you have a relation-ship with God through Jesus Christ? Do you be-lieve you are the sinner Christ died for? Have you ever thanked Him personally for that and invited Christ into your life? If not, use the prayer in the Food For Thought section. If you have, spend a moment thanking Him.

3 minutes

2. (On your own) Look up these two verses and meditate on them:
   □ 1 Thessalonians 5:17
   □ Matthew 6:6
   Pray about them now on your own or with your group. Thank Him for hearing your prayers.

1 minute

3. (In twos) Discuss a "Nehemiah prayer" (a "Help!" prayer) you have prayed and God has answered or one you need to pray! Praise or pray together. Thank Him He has heard your prayers.

5 minutes

4. (As a group) Pray:
   □ for people like Cornelius who are good people looking for God.
   □ God will make you like Daniel and Nehemi-ah—strong in prayer and determined to follow through with your prayertime.
   □ God will make the believers in your fellowship desert disciples like John the Baptist and Paul.

6 minutes

5. (In twos) Share with a partner or in small groups where your prayer life is at the moment. Rate it on a scale of 1–10. Then pray around the group for each other, using short sentences and conver-sational prayer.

5 minutes

•DIGGING DEEPER•

Nehemiah

1. Study each passage and list characteristics of Nehemiah's prayer life.

   Nehemiah 1:1-11

   He mourned, fasted, and prayed when up against catastrophe.
   He begins by describing God, i.e., awesome, etc.
   He asks God to listen.

   Nehemiah 2:1-6

   He prayed to God before Asking the king to rebuild the city.

   Nehemiah 3:1-2

   Act of consecration

   Nehemiah 4:1-5

   Nehemiah 4:7-9

   Prayed to God so they would not be Attacked

   Nehemiah 5:19

   He asks God to remember him for All the good he did for Isreal

Nehemiah 6:1-9 — vs. 9

Lord strengthen my hands, Nehemiah says

Nehemiah 6:10-14

He prayed for those who wanted to kill him.

Nehemiah 8:1-6

All the people blessed God! — All together

Nehemiah 9:1-37

A powerful God — Describes lots of things God and did

Nehemiah 13:14, 22, 29, 31

vs. 14 — Remember me God, vs. Remember me & spare me

Continuously asking God to remember him.

2. What patterns can you identify in Nehemiah's prayers? (Look for repetition of style, attitude, words, or ideas.)

Humble, patient, forgiving, listens to God

3. From his prayers, describe Nehemiah's God.

Powerful God, merciful God, protecting God

4. What national sins do we need to confess to the Lord?

Abortion, Pornography, drugs, murder Liberalism

5. Describe your prayer life. How does it compare with Nehemiah's? What changes would you like to make with God's help and His Spirit's enabling?

I need to trust God more - that's what Nehemiah did.

6. Is your view of God as grand as Nehemiah's? What will you do this week to enhance it?

Somewhat, I know it in my head, but not my heart

For Further Study

1. Begin each morning this week by writing down God's agenda and priorities for your day. Check your list at the end of the day to see if you have accomplished His will.
2. In a journal, record a personal prayer using one of Nehemiah's as a model.

•TOOL CHEST•
(A Suggested Optional Resource)

WITH MY WHOLE HEART

Nehemiah was a man who stood for truth and for what was right in the midst of criticism and adversity. Against all odds he led a delegation back to his homeland to perform an incredible feat: rebuilding Jerusalem's wall. This took tremendous discipline and dependence on God for daily enabling to meet the opposition and to accomplish the task. Nehemiah was a man of tough moral fiber and inner strength. The discipline of his prayer life is the reason why he could stand up to the challenges and evils of his times.

With My Whole Heart (Multnomah), by Karen Mains, has been written for the purpose of helping today's Christian woman: develop character, consistency, and commitment; make godly "personal, spiritual, and ethical choices"; love God with her whole being as Nehemiah did. The reader will be refreshed and revived by the following chapters.

8. On Being Edited: The Discipline of Welcoming Corrections
9. The God Hunt: The Discipline of Finding God in Every Day
10. Prison on Our Backs: The Discipline of Choosing Freedom from the Need for Human Approval
12. Handmaidens: The Discipline of Offering Myself Up

2
Praise

[handwritten notes in left margin: Praise - Exalting God for what He's done!! Worship - Exalting God for what is - done it is - for who He IS!]

[handwritten notes in right margin: PrAISe / Repentance / Ask for others / Yourself]

•FOOD FOR THOUGHT•

"Where there is no vision, the people perish."
—Proverbs 29:18

In one of my husband's books, he gives a simple pattern for prayer: P for praise, R for repentance, A for asking for others, and Y for asking for yourself. He says praise is where we should start. Most of us reverse the whole procedure and "YARP" instead! If you check on your prayer time, this is probably the case. To praise or worship means to ascribe value or worth to an object—in other words, "worthship." For a person to be able to praise his God means he must believe the object of his faith is worthy of his praise. Therefore, it follows that the more he knows about the object, the more praise he will want to express!

The whole duty of man is to glorify God. Psalm 50:23 says, "Whoso offereth praise glorifies . . . God."

If we would learn to pray, we must first learn to praise. And if we would learn to praise, we must first have a true vision and some understanding of the true God. Although God is invisible, He chose to reveal Himself in many ways, one of which was to show a small glimpse of His glory through mystical visions. The result was a spontaneous and sincere acknowledgment of His worth by those most honored people who received such revelations, and a corresponding sense of their own unworthiness. We can share in these mystical visions as we read those particular passages of Scripture in our prayer time and meditate on what it was that these men saw. Think about the verbal pictures they drew for us and look for any aspect of what they saw that has significance. For example, Isaiah 6:1 says, "In the year that King Uzziah died I saw the Lord seated on a throne, high and exalted, and the train of His robe filled the temple." This reminds us of the position of the Lord—high above all.

A vision of God results in a vision of ourselves. It cuts us down to size and gives us true perspective.

Another way we can have a vision of God is by studying the Scriptures. We can begin to understand His worth through a realization of His character in the revelation of the Old Testament, and further as we watch Him in action through the Gospel narratives. It is through the Bible, then, that we can come to know how much we have to praise God for—not only His being, but His doing. We can cultivate praise by fixing our hearts on God (Ps. 57:7) and by meditating on His ways and works. It is, however, through quiet contemplation of His work on the cross for us that praise can best be born.

Prayer, then, *must* commence with praise. However, some people today tend to take the expression of praise to an extreme. I personally react negatively toward bright, shiny Christians telling me they have learned to praise God for anything from leukemia to a divorce! How can we praise God for those things He weeps over? On earth Jesus wept at death, was angry about the hardness of people's hearts which caused divorce, and condemned those who exploited the weak. Perhaps what these modern "praisers" are really trying to say is that it is possible to find God in every dark situation. To see Him high and lifted up and to praise Him for who He is and for what we can learn of Him in the dark circumstances is not to praise Him for the darkness itself!

A friend who has been a missionary in France for a long time told me of an extremely difficult set of circumstances that led her to inquire of a fellow worker, "How can you be so serene when everything has collapsed around you?" "Well," the fellow missionary replied, "when I can't praise God for what He allows, I can always praise Him for who He is 'in' what He has allowed." That helps. Try it!

Another good reason for praising God is that praise keeps the credit where it is due. Remember, he who offers praise glorifies God. I'll never forget doing a Bible study on the crowns that will be the rewards in heaven for faithful Christians. What an exciting discovery it was for me to see the good things awaiting us in eternity—rewards for such things as hospitality, martyrdom, evangelistic effort, and even a reward for those who "look for His coming." That last one should be easy to win!

I began to have a vision of God patting my head as He piled on the crowns, the weight of which surely would give me an eternal headache! There I would be, sitting smugly in heaven with all that gold giving me justified glory! Well, that didn't sound quite right, so I began to think again. Not one reward would I ever receive that had been obtained without His enabling, His gifts, or His grace. Not one victory won that He had not fought for me, not one soul brought to life without the regenerating operation of the Holy Spirit. Not one. Not one!

As I read Revelation 5, I saw the twelve elders representing (some believe) the church. Sitting around that glorious Being on the throne, they appeared to be well and truly crowned. What then? Seeing the Lord high and lifted up and His train filling the temple brought the only possible response. Rising, they fell on their faces and cast their crowns at His feet where they truly belonged.

I decided that day I would not wait till I sat in glory. If men ever gave me a crown, I would cast it at His feet. It would be His anyway.

One day I was asked to address a meeting for the Fellowship of Christian Athletes. Sportsmen and women from all over the country would be there, together with their coaches, wives, husbands, and family members. They would gather together for one glorious week-end of fellowship. Since in those days I was struggling with my ability to speak to mixed groups, I found I desperately wanted a crown of approval from those men. I knew how hard it was for some of them to be spoken to by a "mere woman." I wanted so badly to do a good job! Then I read Revelation 5 again on my knees.

At the end of my talk, I told the group about my struggles. I shared with them that I had cast that particular crown at His feet *before* I came to the podium. It didn't matter anymore. All that mattered was the coal from the altar, spoken of in Isaiah 6. He had touched my lips and demanded my obedience to "go for Him." Why, then, should I look for a crown? *His* is the command, *His* the enabling, *His* the cleansing, *His* the message, and if any blessing, *His* the praise. Men could give what they would—or wouldn't. All that mattered was that the *Lord* be high and lifted up.

Praise enables us to keep ourselves in true perspective and give credit where it is due. Praise ye the Lord! And hallelujah!

On a practical note, none of this will work unless we take the time and trouble to prepare our week to include an appointment with God. With our busy schedules, this is sometimes easier said than done!

26

When I was a young missionary mother, we lived in a small house. It was the sort of place that made you feel as if you had at least 50 children, when you knew for a fact you had only three! We shared our home with various people whom God sent into our lives, and we enjoyed what could best be described as "close" fellowship. In fact, if a definition of fellowship is "two fellows in a ship," we felt as though there were 100 fellows all in the same vessel!

At that time all of our children were under school age, and we were enjoying a typical English winter, which was good for ducks but a bit damp for human beings. Thus we were all confined indoors for days on end. I remember reading Matthew 6:6 and feeling desperate: "But when you pray, go into your room, close the door and pray to your Father, who is unseen. Then your Father, who sees what is done in secret, will reward you." The only places in our house that were secret were the closets, but they were so full of clothing, children's toys, and junk that it required fortitude just to open one of them. There had to be a place somewhere, I remember thinking. Just a space I could be "apart," untouchable by sticky fingers or a crawling baby. Away from the teen-age problems with our lodgers—just for a *few* minutes!

Then my eye lighted on the children's playpen. It was ideal. So I got *in* and put them *out!* Of course the little imps started rattling the bars furiously to get at me. (As far as I can remember, that's the only time they tried to get in instead of escaping!) But I was safe. It was a little oasis of space. Just a few mind-saving moments so that I could share some "secrets" with the Father and receive some encouragement from Him. Then I was ready for the battle again as I clambered ungracefully, but renewed, out of my open-air closet!

I don't care how small your house is, or how noisy the kids, there will be a place. Find it! Name it! Tell Jesus you'll see Him there! Prepare—plan a place and time with Him and begin to learn to praise.

→ Good Example

•TALKING IT OVER•

Suggested Times

---

1. WORK TOGETHER.

12 minutes

A description of *how* a man can praise God is given in the Scriptures. Work together in a group or in a notebook on your own.

☐ Soul praise can take place without words; it is an attitude of the mind. Look up the following verses and read them aloud in the group or to yourself.
Psalm 4:7 → gladness
Psalm 103:1 → Bless the Lord
Isaiah 29:13

☐ Social praise. The Spirit of praise is a social spirit. The man who praises God desires to do so publicly. Read the following verses.
Psalm 34:3
Psalm 40:10   *Interesting*

☐ Song praise. The spirit of praise is the spirit of song. In the Old Testament we find lyrical and musical forms of praise as in the Book of Psalms. In the New Testament and today as well psalms, hymns, and spiritual songs are used in praise. Read Ephesians 5:18-20.   *church*

---

2. READ AND DISCUSS TOGETHER.

12 minutes

We don't *need* a mystic vision. We can "see" God through the biblical revelation of His attributes. Look up as many of these verses as possible. Find and write down each attribute of God that is mentioned:

☐ Genesis 17:1 – Almighty
☐ Genesis 21:33 – Everlasting
☐ Exodus 34:6
☐ Joshua 3:10
☐ John 17:25 – Righteous
☐ Romans 15:5 → Gives perseverance/ encouragement
☐ Romans 15:13 → God of hope
☐ Romans 15:33 → God of peace
☐ 1 Corinthians 1:9
☐ 2 Corinthians 1:3

☐ 1 John 4:8
Share your findings with the group.

3. MAKE YOUR OWN ACROSTIC. *6 minutes*
   This is my acrostic of some of the elements that
   help me to praise God. Make your own acrostic.
   Prepare
   Remember
   Adore
   Imagine
   Sing
   Express

Pray
Resued me from Sin/hell
ASK
Invite
State to God
Everlasting

•PRAYING IT THROUGH•

*Suggested
Times*

---

1. (On your own) Read one of the following passages to yourself:
   ☐ Isaiah 6:1-8
   ☐ Ezekiel 1:24-28
   ☐ Daniel 7:9-10
   ☐ Revelation 1:10-16
   Spend some time in silent contemplation and praise. A vision of God brings forth praise. What else does a vision of God do to a person? To find this out, discover what reaction the following men had to their visions.
   ☐ Isaiah 6:5
   ☐ Ezekiel 1:28
   ☐ Daniel 8:18
   ☐ Revelation 1:17

8 minutes

---

2. (As a group) Spend a few moments praising God:
   ☐ for His character or who He is. You may begin one-sentence prayers with: "O Lord, we want to praise You for who You are." One word or one sentence may follow. For example, "Thank You for Your holiness, Lord."
   ☑ for what He has made or His handiwork. Look up and read Psalm 19:1-6. Spend time this week in the Book of Psalms contemplating what God has made.
   ☑ for His power manifest. Read Psalm 77 together or in private. The psalmist is in trouble. What helps him at this time? Write a summary of this psalm.
   ☐ His providence shown. Read Job 38–41 on your own or in pairs.
   ☐ what He has done. We can see God in His loving action toward us in redemption. Choose one of the following passages to read and meditate on.
   Psalm 22:1-23
   Isaiah 50:4-8
   Matthew 26:36-42

8 minutes

Matthew 27:27-32
Matthew 27:33-44
Matthew 27:45-50
John 18:19-24
John 19:1-7
Philippians 2:5-8

Praise God for what He has done for you from each passage. If working in a group, each person should choose a different aspect to praise Him for and spend a few moments in prayer together. When it is hard to praise God for what He allows to happen in our lives, we can praise Him for who He is, what He has made, and what He has done.

---

3. (On your own) Remember one by one some characteristics of your Heavenly Father, or some manifestly loving action of His toward you. Think about a prayer He has answered or gift He has given you. This positive activity will surely help to lift your heart in praise.   *4 minutes*

OPTIONAL
Here are two praise choruses you might use together in your group or on your own:
"Alleluia!" by Gil Moegerle (*Hymnal for Contemporary Christians*, Singspiration Music).
"Holy, Holy" by Jimmy Owens (*Folk Celebration*, Singspiration Music).

Bible Study - Read this Ps. 103

—— Before You Say "Amen" ——

•DIGGING DEEPER•

1. Read Psalm 103. What is the overall theme of the psalm?

   Praise- Blessing God

   Identify the writer's mood or tone (angry, stern, jubilant, nostalgic).

   Jubilant

2. Who is speaking in this psalm? Is there a change of speaker?

   David, No

3. How many calls to praise do you count? Who is being called to praise? What is significant about the location of these calls to praise?

   1) Six 2) us, angels, those who do His will →3) Begins + Ends w/ ✗T
   Soul

4. List all the characteristics of God's nature which are praised in this psalm.

   compassionate, gracious, lovingkindness

5. List the works of God which are praised.

   1. Pardons us, 2. crowns us 3. heals us
   4. satisfies us!

6. What are the natural divisions of the psalm? How did you support your decision?

   1-7- Tells who He is, what He does
   8-14- Tells of compassion, but His love deserts us
   15-19- we are just new, but It's love deserts us
   32
   20-24 Call to Praise

7. Record repeating words and phrases. Do these have any bearing on your answer to question one?

Bless the Lord

8. What examples of God's love and compassion does the psalmist cite?

1. Compassion on us, 2. remove our sins
3. slow to anger 4. Abounding in loving kindness

9. Give examples from your own life of God's love and compassion.

He puts up w/ me

10. From your study of Psalm 103, describe how God feels about His people.

He loves us, + is worthy to be praised

When would it be appropriate to recall this psalm?

When Satan is telling us we are scum!

11. What are the conditions for receiving God's love and compassion? Are you lacking in meeting any of these conditions? What will you do about your deficiency?

1. Accepting it

12. Compose your own prayer of praise incorporating the elements you observed in this psalm.

God you're great, I love you, thanks for who you are + what you've done

For Further Study
1. Memorize Psalm 103:1-5. Review these verses with a friend.
2. With the help of a commentary, identify an earlier Old Testament incident/passage of which Psalm 103 is reminiscent.

•TOOL CHEST•
(A Suggested Optional Resource)

PSALMS

Derek Kidner's four volume commentary is published by InterVarsity Press. This work introduces the Bible student to the rich spiritual nuggets from the Psaltry. It explains the various categories of psalms and which pertains to the one under study, the historical references from which they draw upon, the likely setting of their composition and use, and how each structure contributes to its beauty and message.

3

In Jesus' Name

Key Pts.
- Enter His presence we must pray in Jesus' Name not any — body elses
- Heb. 4: 14-16 — Concentrate on this

N. today

•FOOD FOR THOUGHT•

It's not difficult to see what God has to do with prayer. He is the One who has the wherewithal to deliver the answers. Yet Jesus Christ's part in it all is a little more difficult to understand. In fact, many people say it is not even necessary to bring Him into it. They say you can go straight to God without invoking the name of Jesus. But the Bible teaches us that we cannot just blast off into the very presence of God. We must not ignore the signs that instruct us to enter into that fantastic throne room in a prescribed way.

Not long ago I had to have some tests at the hospital. My doctor gave me a note, which I carefully clutched to me as I approached the gate. In his name I announced my arrival. There was no way I could obtain my conference with the surgeon without that note signed by my doctor's own hand. I was then instructed to follow a yellow line on the floor that would eventually lead me to the inner office of the specialist who would listen to my problem, diagnose the disease, and prescribe a remedy. I would never have tried to find my own way or take an unauthorized route. Neither did I think of throwing away the name of my doctor who sent me to the surgeon, with all of his authority behind that interview. I was in a different world. The medical world was totally strange and unfamiliar, and who was I to know better than the principalities who ruled that sphere? Following the instructions carefully, I arrived in front of the big man himself. He read my doctor's note, smiled, and gently began to ask me many questions. I was so scared and nervous. If only my doctor was there to be with me and explain my case. Suddenly the door opened and there he was! Knowing my justified fear, he had come himself to be with me.

Jesus Christ said, "I am the way and the truth and the life. No one comes to the Father except through Me" (John 14:6). The note I hold in my hand has my disease on it—sin and selfishness. It is signed by my Jesus in His own blood; and, following His instructions, I approach the inner room where God is, the way He told me to. He said, "You may ask Me for anything in My name, and I will do it" (John 14:14). Therefore, in His name I come, and God receives me for His sake, for Jesus is none other than the second person of the Godhead. With all of His authority behind me, I dare to follow the arrows and find myself in a conference that begins to deal with my human malady. Feeling frightened in that inner place, I suddenly see Him—He is there to explain my case for me. What a relief! So you see, a vision of God is needed, but a vision of Christ is necessary too.

Because man's attitude toward prayer is often unbelievably arrogant, he needs to understand that he can't just saunter in "upstairs" any time he wants to. Even if he thinks God will almost fall out of heaven in His eagerness to grant his request and keep him happy, he has to be willing to have his ignorance exposed and learn some facts.

Now if we approach the High and Holy One with the attitude, "Here I am. I've come my own way, not Yours, and You'd better be grateful," I venture to suggest we've not had a true vision of God at all. If, on the other hand, we have begun to cultivate an attitude of intelligent praise, we will leave behind our small-minded ignorance and grasp God's relationship with Christ where prayer is concerned. Having begun to understand His character, we will then be asking, "How can I possibly come near a Being as holy as this?" Apart from some authority who explains my presence and states my case, I will surely be tongue-tied, nervous, and extremely conscious of my unworthiness.

Maybe some of us, realizing all this and acquiescing to the brightness of His presence, feel we might better send our prayers via some super-saint, who could survive the proximity of holiness and deliver them for us. The more we come to know God, the more the concept of a mediator—that is, someone who will stand in between us and God and speak on our behalf—becomes an obvious necessity.

Some of us go to the antithesis of arrogance and decide God is too busy to be bothered with such human trivia. Overconscious of our inadequacy, we bury our heads in our hands and duck behind the wooden church pew, whispering furtively toward the floor. We may

[handwritten marginalia: Jesus knows how we pray, because He lived here — He was here in the flesh, yet did not sin]

wonder if some holy angel will find those needy words and bear them up, winging them toward the throne room—but we doubt it. How can He understand me anyway? If prayer is sharing my heart with someone who can understand my earthly problems, maybe it would be more practical to pray to another human being instead of a divine Spirit who does not know the feelings of the infirmities of my fallen humanity. Unless, of course, God could know what it is to be a man; then He would know how hard it is down here—"here" being the place I live and struggle, puzzle, and fail.

But He became a man, didn't He? And that's what it's all about. We *have* a Mediator who lived on earth and now lives forever in heaven. There is a perfect human being in glory—His name is Jesus, our Saviour and Intercessor.

Daniel saw Him in the very throne room with God. That vision must have given him a terrific shock. I'm sure whatever else he was expecting, he wasn't expecting to see a man in heaven.

The vision Daniel saw was a vision of One like a Son of man receiving a kingdom, an eternal kingdom, from the hand of the Father. We know who that Man was, don't we? He was the pre-incarnate Son of God. What priceless comfort to know there is a Man in glory.

In Exodus days God taught His people a very simple lesson. It was this—they would need a holy man, called a priest, to present their petitions to God. He would meet them at the door of the tabernacle and receive their sacrifice for sin and their prayer requests, then he would pray for them. *[handwritten: → how it used to be ←]*

The tabernacle—God's graphic visual aid in the wilderness—was the meeting place for sinful man and holy God. There was a place within it called the holy of holies, which housed the law written on tables of stone. This was covered with the mercy seat. Here God had promised to meet with His people. The holiness of God required a careful approach into His presence. Instructions had to be followed, and the rules were meticulously given by God to Moses, who gave them to the people. *[handwritten: → once a year!]*

Once a year the great high priest was allowed to enter the "holiest of all," bringing with him the sacrifice for the sin of the nation. The sacrifice was in the form of a young and perfect lamb which had just been slain, prefiguring the Lamb of God who would take away the sin of the world. Blood would be sprinkled on that empty mercy seat, a reminder that a life must be shed if there was to be an "atonement" between sinful man and holy God. Only by the shedding of blood could there be remission or forgiveness of sin. What sin? The sin of breaking those Ten Commandments of this holy God encased in the ark of promise underneath the mercy seat.

Even the way into the "holiest of all" was cut off from the sinner by a heavy curtain or veil. Now we know when the Lamb of God did appear to put away sin once and for all, by the sacrifice of Himself, that the veil was rent in two and a way was opened into the very presence of God. Presenting Himself to the Ancient of Days as the supreme and adequate sacrifice for the sin of the whole world, Jesus was accepted by the Father and He sat down on that empty mercy seat, which is His throne in heaven (Heb. 8:1-2). It is the place where justice and mercy meet for you and for me. It is the place where my Saviour, both Lamb and Priest, sits to receive me for an audience with the King. The throne is close to the ear of God, and the Scriptures tell me plainly that He ever lives to make intercession for me. No longer do I need an earthly priest to take my prayer into God's presence. I have Jesus, my great High Priest, who has passed into the heavens for me. We can read Hebrews 4:14-16 in the Scriptures about this.

There are four things that we can learn from these passages about the prayer work Jesus our great High Priest is accomplishing on our behalf. *First* of all, we know He *sympathizes* with us. How do we know this?

I always believed that Jesus was touched by my infirmities, but I never realized before that He was actually touched by the very *feelings* of my infirmities. Sometimes I really believe no one, not even those closest to me, can understand how I feel. I can try to explain, but the words don't come out right; and sometimes I don't even understand myself, so that I can explain me! I only know I suffer agonies no one seems to understand.

Now then, Jesus my great High Priest has been there because He was taken from among men. He can truly have compassion because He has "felt" my feelings. He knows; He cares; He understands. He is touched with the very feeling of my infirmities; therefore, I can come boldly to the throne of grace. And when I come to Him, what will He give me?

Well, *second*, we find we have a High Priest who supplies. Supplies what? Mercy and grace to help us in our time of need. What is the difference between mercy and grace? Mercy doesn't give us everything we deserve; grace gives us what we don't deserve.

Some time ago Stuart was explaining the difference between justice, mercy, and grace, using a helpful illustration. When Pete, our youngest, was small, he needed disciplining for a breach of family

38

law. As he was asked to bend over so Stuart could apply the board of education to his seat of learning, Pete said, "Hurry up, Dad, 'cause I don't believe this is going to hurt you as much as it does me!" After five out of the prescribed ten whacks had been administered for the just reward of his deeds, his dad stopped. "Why have you stopped, Dad?" inquired Pete. "Because I have mercy on you," replied his father. "Justice gives you all you've asked for, while mercy doesn't give you all you deserve!" Pete went to his room to contemplate the proceedings, and soon his dad called upstairs to ask if he'd like to go for some ice cream with him. What was that? Well, that was grace. Grace gives you what you don't deserve!

We have a High Priest who understands us perfectly because He was tempted in every way we are, yet without sin. Therefore we come boldly to the throne room, knowing we will receive mercy. This is a sharp and true reminder of our sinful nature, yet grace to help with the repercussions of that deceitful heart of ours. This we don't deserve at all! So when my time of need comes, I know where my help can be found—in the throne room. Remember, God has given everything to His Son. In Christ are all the heavenly resources necessary to help me in my time of need. I will be supplied with a quality of divine help that is eternal. It never loses its value; it is called grace, and it is dispensed by the Son of God from the mercy seat in the "holiest of all."

Third, Christ is a High Priest who saves us. There are, basically, three aspects of our salvation: He has saved us from our sins, He is saving us now from our selfishness, and He will save us from judgment when we face Him in eternity.

In the *King James Version,* Hebrews 7:25 says, "He is able to save them to the uttermost." As a street preacher once put it, He is able to save from "the guttermost to the uttermost." No matter to what depths we have sunk, no matter how great our need, or how fast sin or habit holds us, *He is able.* Not only is He able to save us to the uttermost, He is willing; and not only is He willing, He is praying to the Father on our behalf for our release. He longs to release the supply of strength and grace that we need in order to overcome. He waits for us to ask Him to do just that through prayer.

Lastly, Jesus is the High Priest who is seated. Where is He seated? Hebrews 8:1-2 tells us that He is seated on the right hand of the throne of the Majesty in heaven. He is our Mediator, the only One we need. We must approach God through Him, for the Ancient of Days has given Him the authority of the kingdom, and we can only be accepted in the Beloved.

This is perhaps new and difficult ground for you. Until we come to realize there is a Man in glory, who is Jesus, our great High Priest, who ever lives to make intercession for us, we will never come boldly before the throne. When we realize the veil was rent for us—the veil being His flesh (Heb. 10:20)—then we know He cares and prays for us. When we think about His prayers, we have to realize He is desirous of saving us now—He died for that reason. But also we realize He lives to save us now—He was raised for that reason! I can come in His name and for His sake, because of His saving work on my behalf; and I can come knowing I shall be supplied from the throne room with grace to help in my time of need.

Heb. 7:25

Jesus is praying for us, this the Bible teaches. We have learned some of the things He is praying. Now let me ask you a question: Is He seeing His prayers answered in your life?

Key Question

Are Gods Prayers for you being Answered In your life

If we are living Colossians 3:17 - Gods prayers for our lives will be Answered

•TALKING IT OVER•

1. READ AND DISCUSS.
   Look up Daniel 7:13-14 and write in your note-book or share in discussion a description of the scene in heaven.

   7 minutes

2. READ AND SHARE.
   ☐ Read Hebrews 4:14-16. Verbalize to the group or describe in your notebook what you think this is saying.
   ☐ Read Hebrews 5:1-2 and answer: How do we know our Lord is sympathetic to us?
   ☐ In your own words, sum up Jesus' feelings about us as found in Hebrews 4:15.

   8 minutes

3. ANSWER QUESTIONS IN PAIRS.
   Work on the following questions in pairs or in your notebook. Share your findings if in a class or group.
   ☐ Read Hebrews 7:23-26. What is the difference between our heavenly High Priest Jesus and an earthly human one such as Aaron?
   ☐ What does Christ ever live to do for us? (v. 25)
   ☐ How can we be sure God hears the prayers of our great High Priest? (v. 26)
   ☐ In verse 25 we read a statement of His ability on our behalf. Verbalize it to your partner or write it in your own words in your notebook.

   7 minutes

4. STUDY TOGETHER.
   Study together through these passages of Scripture. Discuss or make notes.
   ☐ Read Hebrews 8:1-2. How is Jesus described here?
   ☐ Read Hebrews 8:5. What was the earthly counterpart of the tabernacle in the heavens?
   ☐ Read Hebrews 9:8. What was the Holy Spirit saying about the holiest of all through this visual aid of the Old Testament?
   ☐ Read Hebrews 8:8-13. If the high priest's work

   8 minutes

was to mediate to the Father for the people, then Jesus, our heavenly minister and mediator, ever lives to do just that for us (1 John 2:1). What is Jesus praying for us? Make a list of Jesus' prayer requests on our behalf.

☐ Read Hebrews 10:19-25. These verses tell us that there are three things beginning with "let us" that we need to do. Name them.

•PRAYING IT THROUGH•

Suggested Times

1. (On your own) Spend some time in silent prayer. Be very still and come into the throne room. See Jesus, your great High Priest, there for you. Come boldly to the Father in His name. Thank Him that the veil of His flesh was rent for you. Ask what you will. Remember, He sympathizes, supplies, and saves; and because He is seated in glory, He has the power to work on your behalf. Thank Him. Leave your request with God. Jesus will pray about it too!

5 minutes

2. (As a group) Pray for:
   ☑ Someone you know who is being tempted. Using their first names only (or change the names to protect them), pray He who was also tempted (He sympathizes) will deliver them.
   ☑ Specific members of your family who are in times of need. We have a High Priest who provides mercy and grace to help us (He supplies) in times of need.
   ☐ Someone in dire straights financially, physically, spiritually, or psychologically. "He is able to save to the uttermost" (He saves).

10 minutes

3. (On your own) Meditate on this truth: He is "seated" in glory.

5 minutes

•DIGGING DEEPER•

1. Study the phrase "in the name of Jesus" within each of its contexts. Do you see a theology developing? What do these passages teach about Jesus' name? What is the particular emphasis in each?

Matthew 18:19-20

Two or three agreeing | binding loosing

Matthew 24:4-5

Many will claim to be Jesus don't be deceived

Mark 9:38-41

Serving in Jesus Name, casting out demons in Jesus Name

John 14:12-14   - IJN.5:14- Principal

Ask Anything in Jesus' name it will be done

John 16:19-24

Asking / Receiving

Acts 2:21

In Jesus's name we are Saved call on Him He'll save us

Acts 4:12

No other name we are saved under

Acts 10:43

Receive forgiveness of sins

Romans 10:9-13

Salvation in Jesus' Name

Philippians 2:9-10

Gods Name is Above All

Colossians 3:17

Everything we do, do in the Name of Jesus! word or deed

Hebrews 1:4

God is Above Angels

James 5:14-15

Healing In Jesus' Name

1 John 5:13

Eternal life in Jesus' Name

2. Is it enough to simply utter the name of Jesus in our prayers? Will this assure us of an affirmative answer? Doesn't this seem like a gimmick? What else is required according to your study?

Faith, persistence, must be His will

3. With what must our requests, petitions, supplications, and intercessions be consistent?

God's Will

4. Who answers the prayer said in Jesus' name?

God

5. What do these verses indicate concerning the authority of Christ Jesus?

Alot of it, He controls it

6. Read Acts 3:1-10. What does Peter demonstrate he had learned about prayer? What is interesting about the time of day the healing took place?

In the afternoon, D Jesus' Name the man walked Again

7. In Acts 3:11-16 Peter explains how the miracle transpired. What two elements were essential for the crippled man's "complete healing"?

Faith, & Name of Jesus

Are these two elements crucial to your prayers? Have you grown slack in either one: acknowledging the supremacy and authority of Christ and aligning your requests with His purposes; or exercising faith in His ability to accomplish all things which are in agreement with His good and perfect will?

8. Peter was willing in Acts 4:8-12 to testify before many important and notable people of his dedication to Jesus Christ of Nazareth. He attributed to the Lord Jesus the crippled man's healing. Are you willing to acknowledge your commitment to Jesus before important people in your life, and to tell of His marvelous works?

   Yes — Are we no matter what the cost?

9. What were the responses made by the officials to Peter's witness? (Acts 4:13-22)

   v. 13 — *Astonished*

   v. 14 — *Nothing they could say*

   v. 18 — *Commanded them not to preach, speak in the name of Jesus*

   v. 21

10. Where did Peter and John get their courage? (Acts 4:23-31) Do you think they ever felt frightened or intimidated? How did they cope with and combat these feelings? To whom would the Lord Jesus have you witness? Will you?

    God gave them courage. | Yes, they were humans | God's grace | People at work, yes

11. Write a heart-to-heart prayer below to the Lord about this matter. Recite it each day of next week and expect an opportunity to acknowledge Jesus before men. Make sure you go in His name.

    Lord, help me to be a witness for you, help me Lord to be courageous, + strong! Amen

For Further Study
1. Memorize John 14:12-14.
2. Write out an imaginary conversation with a friend with the purpose of explaining to your friend what Christ Jesus means to you.

•TOOL CHEST•
(A Suggested Optional Resource)

ON HOLY GROUND

On Holy Ground is another inductive Bible study on prayer by Kirkie Morrissey (NavPress). It is topical in nature and focuses on the ingredients, hindrances, results, and methods of prayer. It emphasizes the importance of allowing Scripture to set the standards of our prayer life. This book can be used for personal quiet times or by small groups. Additional questions for small group discussion are included at the end of each chapter.

4
Jesus' Prayers

• FOOD FOR THOUGIIT •

We are fortunate to have two prayers of our Lord recorded for us in John 17 and Matthew 26. They are not prayers He told us to pray, but actual accounts of the words He spoke in prayer *on our behalf*.

I suppose that to listen to a man's prayers is to listen to and see into the real person he is. One feels almost embarrassed at the privilege of hearing a man bare his soul before God. John 17 is an unbelievably beautiful and practical prayer that the disciples experienced on their behalf. Their time of defeat in Gethsemane seems all the more sad in light of it!

Apparently Jesus made a habit of praying aloud. This was not for His benefit, that He might corral His wandering thoughts, but for our benefit! How do we know this? Look up John 11:41-42. If His audible prayers are indeed for "the people who stand by," may we who stand by listening to the words of His prayers today believe God sent Him and place our confidence in His manifest willingness to answer prayer!

In John 17, Jesus prays for His disciples. "I pray for them. I am not praying for the world, but for those You have given Me, for they are Yours. . . . My prayer is not for them alone. I pray also for those who will believe in Me through their message" (John 17:9, 20). Doesn't this make you want to listen in to His prayers?

Even in His final agony of prayer in Gethsemane before the Crucifixion, we find our Lord Jesus praying desperately for Himself, and yet never able to divorce Himself from concern for His beloved disciples. Oh, that we might learn such unselfishness as we pray for ourselves. However, He does solicit the prayer watch of His closest friends in His extremity.

Can you imagine what it must be like to have God tell you that He's feeling "heavy" and very depressed? (Matt. 26:38) That in itself is mind-boggling. But then to /be asked to respond to the divine request, "Stay here and keep watch with Me"! Surely His closest and dearest human friends would gladly and willingly fall to their knees, vowing to keep alert and responsive to His need. What a privilege to support the Son of God as He battled with the forces of hell that were seeking to oppose His decision to die!

It is rather surprising therefore to hear the snores emanating from the disciples in Matthew 26:40! "But they were tired," you say. True, but so was Jesus. Tired of loving, giving, healing, caring, teaching, admonishing, and warning these men! Do you ever get tired of telling people the same thing over and over again when no response is forthcoming? There is nothing quite so frustrating as seeking to move the unmovable or shake the unshakable out of their complacency. "Watch and pray; there's a cross tomorrow," the Son of God had warned loud and clear that very night!

The problem with the disciples at this particular point in time was that they had no sense of ministry to Christ. The ministry of prayer on His behalf was requested of them by Jesus, and they simply snored their response. But don't be too hard on them. What about us? How many times do people who are depressed ask us specifically to pray for them? "Of course we will," we reply. And then we snore our way happily through their crisis hours! We need to think of Jesus' statement: "Whatever you did for one of the least of these brothers of mine, you did for Me" (Matt. 25:40). Forgive us, Lord! If we could grasp the sheer privilege of "doing it unto Him," it would become a precious Gethsemane experience, enabling the oppressed to yield to the will of the Father and us to rejoice in the powerful ministry of supporting prayer.

It is interesting to note that Jesus engaged in prayer even when He did not feel like it. When we are depressed, prayer is not the likeliest of our chosen pastimes. J. Sidlow Baxter, speaking at a booksellers' convention, used the following illustration. He said that the times we feel least like praying, we must take "will" by the hand, leaving our emotions behind! Mr. Will and you must then pray. Day after day this discipline must continue until one day, one emotion may say to the other, "Come on, we're not going to stop them; we may as well go along!"

If Jesus had come to His decision of obedience via the dictation of His emotions, it may well have been a depressed and wrong decision! But Mr. Will and Jesus prayed together in Gethsemane and agreed to allow the Father's will to be done, even though the emotions were dictating otherwise. How great it is that we can *decide* to do God's will when it's the last thing in the world we *want* to do!

Some people tend to think of prayer as a rope attaching a huge ship to a little boat. They are the boat, and the big ship is God's will. They think the rope of prayer is to be used to pull the big ship alongside their little boat. This is against all natural laws, just as it is against all spiritual laws to say, "Not Thy will but mine be done!" Obviously, what has to happen as we pull on the rope of obedience in prayer is that the little boat draws alongside the big ship and sails wherever the big ship wills.

Jesus was depressed and tired as well. But even though He was tired, He was master of His physical body. I think we pamper ourselves dreadfully. "I must get eight hours sleep or I'm no good for the Lord," I heard a lady say not long ago. There are certain times in our lives when the cross must be faced, and no amount of physical strength will equip us for that challenge. Spiritual resources are needed. Surely Jesus required a good night's sleep before being crucified! You might think He would have just excused Himself from the party early, curled up on some moss under His favorite olive tree, and made sure He was ready for the challenge! But read the schedule of the hours preceding the Crucifixion and realize how tired Christ must have been before it had even begun.

Next, Jesus links prayer with the overcoming of temptation. If Jesus needed that Gethsemane prayer time, it goes without saying that we do! And we need it when the crowd is singing hosannahs! Don't be deceived; crowds change, and we don't know if there will be a hostile group and a cross tomorrow. There will be some opportunity to die to our selfishness, that is for sure; and to overcome that test we need to be prepared!

As I read this passage of Scripture, I cannot believe the concern of the Lord Jesus! With all that He had on His mind, He kept coming back to shake His dopey disciples awake—all to no avail. Then it was too late. The crowd was back; the hosannahs had gone, and in their place the discordant notes of hatred and hostility were heard. We see Judas approaching His Master in cold anger, giving Him his kiss of death, and we hear Jesus' response: *"Friend!"* Friend? Yes, the Man who taught the Sermon on the Mount was beautifully demonstrating His own revolutionary teaching—"Love your enemies, do good to those who hate you, bless those who curse you, pray for those who mistreat you" (Luke 6:27-28). Judas, Judas, why

51

are you doing this? Friend! See Jesus reaching out—this is what you do when you've watched and prayed your way through to deciding the will of God is all there is left to do!

Now then, let us have a look at the sleepy students. Peter is on his feet. He has a sword in his hand. Peter has not watched and prayed, and the test has come. We see him fail it with a resounding *F*. Descending on Malchus, who appeared to have a very tempting cranium, Peter decided to make him into twins! That's what happens when you snore your time away. You don't "reach out" like Jesus, you "strike out" like Peter and do damage to the one you have been given the opportunity to love.

Maybe an unexpected incident in the "crowd" at the office turns their hosannahs into hostility. Maybe it is aimed at you! Do you say "friend"—overcoming evil with good? Or do you "cut off their ear" by an unkind, slashing remark? Does your self-defense mechanism spring into play as Peter's did, or are you concerned about the opposition's ear and soul, as Jesus obviously was? I wonder if Malchus' restored hearing affected his heart after Christ's merciful touch? We will know one day, won't we!

"Friend, why have you come?" Jesus asked Judas. What a contrast to Peter's panic plunge! When and how did Jesus do it? He did it when He was tired and very depressed. He did it when He didn't feel like doing it. That's *when* He did it. He went on in importunate prayer, praying the same words until He had pulled Himself in agony alongside His Father's will. That's *how* He did it. He did it with a sense of ministry, honesty, and agony, demonstrating a sense of victory!

When Judas comes tomorrow, what will you call him? What will you do? It will all depend on what happens today in Gethsemane.

•TALKING IT OVER•

---

1. READ AND REVIEW.   *5 minutes*
   Read John 17:1-4, Jesus' prayer for Himself.
   □ What were the two things Jesus was able to say
     He had accomplished in His life on earth?
     (v. 4)
   □ What was the work He had come to do? (vv. 2-
     3) In the light of verse 8, do you think there
     could be any similarity between the work the
     Father gave Jesus to do and the work He has
     given us to do?
   □ What was His prayer for Himself as He faced
     the final accomplishment of that work upon the
     cross? (v. 1)
   □ How then, in the light of my example, Jesus,
     should I be praying for myself?

---

2. DISCUSS AND SHARE.   *5 minutes*
   Discuss the reason we need Jesus our great High
   Priest to pray for us (vv. 11a, 14). Make a list of
   the things He prays for us from the following
   verses in John 17:

v. 11	vv. 21-23
v. 13	v. 24
v. 15	v. 26
v. 17	

   Share your findings with the person next to you in
   the group. Then each one pray for the other about
   these things. Keep your prayers short.

---

3. READ AND ASSIGN.   *10 minutes*
   Read John 17. Assign the following headings to
   corresponding portions of Scripture. (These headings are a summary of some of Christ's requests
   on our behalf.)

JUSTIFIED	SANCTIFIED
PURIFIED	SATISFIED
EDIFIED	UNIFIED
GLORIFIED	

---

4. READ AND WRITE.   *3 minutes*
   Read Matthew 26:36-41. Write out or discuss a
   summary of the Lord's attitude toward tiredness
   at this point.
   □ Where do I stand on this issue?
   □ Am I too easy on myself?

5. IDENTIFY.   *7 minutes*
   Read Matthew 26:36-52 silently. Assign the fol-
   lowing titles to appropriate sections of text they
   describe. (These titles illustrate some of the sen-
   sitivity Christ was seeking to teach His followers
   concerning their prayer life.) Sensitive praying
   includes:
   □ A SENSE OF MINISTRY
   □ A SENSE OF AGONY
   □ A SENSE OF HONESTY
   □ A SENSE OF IMPORTUNITY
   □ A SENSE OF JEOPARDY
   □ A SENSE OF VICTORY

•PRAYING IT THROUGH•

Suggested
Times

1. (On your own) Think about how long Jesus prays for Himself in John 17 and contrast the time He spends praying for us! Surely on that particular night He could have been forgiven for praying for Himself. What an example! Pray we will follow it.

3 minutes

2. (As a group) Circle the prayer request made by Jesus on your behalf that touches you most. "That they (we) may be"

JUSTIFIED   SANCTIFIED
PURIFIED   SATISFIED
EDIFIED   UNIFIED
GLORIFIED

Pray as a group with thanksgiving for these things.

5 minutes

3. (On your own) Pray about your daily "Gethsemane" experience or lack of it. Commit yourself to someone who needs you to "watch and pray" with him or her through his or her crisis hours. Prayer for self cannot be divorced from one's prayer concerns for others.

4 minutes

4. (As a group) Spend time praying you (and your church leaders, missionaries, etc.) will follow the example of Jesus and have a sense of: ministry, agony, honesty, importunity, jeopardy, victory. Pray about the word that you most need to pray about!

8 minutes

•DIGGING DEEPER•

1. What were Jesus' instructions on prayer in each of the following accounts?

   Matthew 5:44
            6:5-8
            6:9-15
            21:13
            21:18-22
   Mark   9:14-29
            11:20-26
            12:40
   Luke   6:28
            18:1-8
            22:39-46

   Review these verses once more and categorize:

   Jesus' commands . . .

   Jesus' promises . . .

   Jesus' warnings . . .

2. What did Jesus model about prayer in each of the following accounts?

   Matthew 6:9-15
            14:23
            19:13
            26:36-46
   Mark   1:35
            14:32-42
   Luke   3:21-23
            6:12-13

9:28-31
22:39-46
John 17

John 17
3. Read John 17. What were Jesus' prayer concerns?

Reflect on the content of your recent prayer concerns.

4. Compare Jesus' prayer requests for Himself with your personal
   prayer requests from this last week.

   Jesus: Mine:

5. Compare Jesus' prayers for His disciples with your prayers for
   your friends and family.

   Jesus: Mine:

6. In what ways does your prayer life resemble that of the Lord
   Jesus? How might you make it more like His?

Matthew 26:36-52
7. Read Matthew 26:36-52. During Jesus' greatest personal struggle we find Him in prayer. What was He saying to the Father,
   asking of His Father, giving to the Father?

8. What obstacles to prayer was Jesus confronted with in Gethsemane?

What obstacles do you face in your prayer times?

What can you learn from Jesus?

9. Begin to pray now that God will prepare you for any future crises, specifically that you might follow Christ's example.

Record your Gethsemane prayer:

For Further Study
1. Keeping in mind Jesus' prayer for His disciples in John 17, begin a prayer journal. Choose one person a week on which to develop a prayer catalog. Write down a prayer for him or her in each of these categories:
Physical welfare
Spiritual welfare
Emotional welfare
Intellectual welfare
Social welfare
Along with each request record a corresponding Bible verse.

•TOOL CHEST•
(A Suggested Optional Resource)

THE FAREWELL DISCOURSE AND FINAL PRAYER OF JESUS
D.A. Carson is a renowned evangelical New Testament scholar. He is true to the NT documents, exegetically sound, and accurately brings the Scriptures to the heart of the lay reader. For further study of Jesus' own prayer and His instructions on prayer, see Carson's exposition of John 17 in *The Farewell Discourse and Final Prayer of Jesus* (Baker). He will help you discover many insights and practical applications for deepening your own prayer life and for imitating that of Christ Jesus.

5
The Conditions of Prayer

•FOOD FOR THOUGHT•

If you purchase a cake mix and begin to put it together, I expect you will follow the instructions on the package. This way you will obtain the desired result. Conditions must be fulfilled if the cake is to look like the picture on the package. But if you decide to do it your own way, tossing all sorts of things into the bowl, then it would be rather foolish to blame the manufacturer for the failure! In the same way, the desired results of prayer can only be obtained if you fulfill the conditions. This is one good reason some prayers are never answered. We just haven't bothered to read the instructions.

But reading the instructions and discovering the conditions can prove to be quite discouraging for a Christian. The more conditions we discover, the more complicated it all seems to become! But don't stop praying! Think of it in the light of relationship. The earthly father receives many requests from his child. He often puts conditions upon the receiver. "If you do such and such, I will give it to you," he may say. Or he may want to know why his child wants a particular item. A good parent must consider many things. Will it benefit the child? Is the child too young to handle it? Would the granted request be more of a blessing if given at a future date? The parent's answer may be *yes*, *no*, or *wait*. Whatever he withholds, it will surely be in love. Our own dear Heavenly Father can be relied on to know what is best for us. And as we grow in our relationship with Him, we begin to understand why He withholds or refuses our petitions. We grow up enough to stop stomping our feet and screaming in rage as He apparently thwarts our desires. In other words, we come to understand the conditions of prayer. So keep praying as you grow in your knowledge of Him.

The Bible talks of many things that hinder our relationship with God. Negative attitudes may prevent God from hearing us. We may still be praying, but we realize He isn't hearing. Why? Let us look at some of those things. The Bible says, "If I had cherished sin in my heart, the Lord would not have listened" (Ps. 66:18). To "cherish sin" is to make sure my prayers remain unanswered, and I may as well get up off my knees and go and deal with it! Confess it. See the people involved, apologize, and "die" to it.

So a bad relationship with God, because of hidden sin, needs to be dealt with *before* we come to prayer. We must always ask God to cleanse our lives from known and unknown sins each time we pray. If sins are known, we must forsake them as thoroughly as a dead man would, for how can those of us who have died to sin live in it any longer? (Rom. 6:2)

Other negative attitudes, which affect our prayers being speedily answered, are those that have to do with relationships within our families (1 Peter 3:6-7).

Negative conditions must be dealt with, but positive commands about prayer must also be fulfilled. Let us look at *faith*—faith in a God we can come to who will reward us. Hebrews 11:6 says, "Without faith it is impossible to please God, because anyone who comes to Him must believe that He exists and that He rewards those who earnestly seek Him."

When I first became a Christian, I thought if I had enough faith to believe God was as big and as great as His holy Word told me He was, then He would reward me. The reward would be the answer to my request, of course! I don't believe this anymore. I most certainly have been rewarded every time I have come to my Father in heaven, trusting Him and acknowledging His ability to help or answer. But the reward has not always been the specific answer I asked for.

To encourage you to have faith in God through prayer does not mean God has to answer your prayer as you outline it to Him. It does mean He will answer it His way, and He Himself will *be* your reward, whatever events happen to surprise you!

Do we have enough faith in the God we petition to tell Him our desire and accept the ensuing situations as His answer? Can we believe in the sovereignty of God enough to trust Him to carry us to the end of the journey all in one piece spiritually, if not physically, along a route we never gave Him permission to take us?

Years ago I rode a motorcycle. One day it refused to start. I left the machine locked up and boarded a bus to take me home. I was busy dreaming about my date for the evening, when the ticket collector inquired if I didn't trust the driver. "Why is that?" I asked, startled. Then I realized I still had my crash helmet on!

There are many crash-helmeted Christians today. They get on the bus of trust through prayer, but expect it to crash at any minute. We need to relax and allow the Driver to take us home by whatever route He chooses—even if it is unfamiliar or dark or spooky! So relax. Trust Him. The ensuing peace is reward indeed.

Often God rewards us with *more* than we ask. For example, we pray He will care for our children. We usually mean for Him to keep them safe physically. Yet sometimes He answers that prayer by allowing physical harm, that their faith may grow spiritually.

God is, of course, interested and concerned about our physical growth and health. When I have to be away from home, I find myself worrying about my children. Sometimes it keeps me awake at night. I imagine everything that *can*, and I am sure *will*, happen to them while I am away. Dialing the phone, I hear it ring—five times! By the time they answer it, I have already had the funeral!

"Oh, Mum," I hear an impatient voice say, "what do you want? We are in the middle of a TV special!" One time, turning to my Bible, I read, "He who watches over Israel will neither slumber nor sleep" (Ps. 121:4). So God said to me, "There's no point in *both* of us lying awake. You sleep; I'll keep!"

Once I slept, and He didn't keep! Or did He? Judy went through a glass window, severing the main tendon in her wrist. Three thousand miles away, I accused God of breaking His promise. "You didn't keep," I sobbed. "You didn't, and I trusted You."

"Oh, but I did," He replied. "I kept her artery from being cut, thus saving her life. I provided her with instant medical expertise and a fine hospital to stay in."
"But I wasn't there," I wailed.

"I was," He replied. "I was her Reward, and now she is safer than she ever was before, spiritually safer, because she has learned I will be with her in whatever valley she must walk through."

And so I learned He rewarded my child with a far richer experience than I had asked for her, and He rewarded me with strength to continue to serve Him thousands of miles away from my hurt little girl! His rewards come in strange wrappings tied with unexpected strings. We look for the familiar, the gift we explicitly ordered from heaven, and receive instead the beautiful surprise packages of God. They are always tied in love by those nail-pierced hands.

You want the promised cake? Then follow the instructions!

•TALKING IT OVER•

1. REVIEW.

   Sin in our tents cannot be hidden from God, for "everything is uncovered and laid bare before the eyes of Him to whom we must give account" (Heb. 4:13). If allowed to remain, sin will affect the whole congregation. One negative condition is known sin in your life.

   5 minutes

2. READ AND WRITE.

   Look up Psalm 66:18 and write it out in your own words. Also read Isaiah 1:15-16. To "regard iniquity" means to allow known sin to remain. An example in the Old Testament is found in the story of Achan.

   5 minutes

3. DISCUSS.

   Look up Joshua 7. Discuss the following questions:
   - ☐ In verses 10-13, God commands Joshua to stop praying. Why?
   - ☐ What has Achan done that deserves death? (v. 13)
   - ☐ How does God tell Joshua to find the culprit? (vv. 14-15)
   - ☐ In verses 19-22 it appears Achan confesses. Why then punish him?

   5 minutes

4. STUDY AND DISCUSS.
   - ☐ Paraphrase 1 Peter 3:6-7. What did Jesus say about this in Matthew 5:23-24? Write out and discuss 1 John 1:5-7.
   - ☐ Two more common attitudes that affect our prayers appear in James 4:2-3. Look them up, write them out in your own words, and then discuss them.

   5 minutes

5. READ, LIST, AND PRAY.
   - ☐ Abiding is another positive condition. Read John 15:7. Write out the promise it contains.

   10 minutes

☐ Make a list of the conditions of abiding from John 15:1-17.

☐ Pray in His name, for His sake, according to His will:

☐ Read John 14:13-14; 15:7, 16; 16:23-24.

☐ Write out what you think it means to pray in His name.

☐ To pray for the right things we need the help of the Holy Spirit, who will tell us what to pray. Look up and read John 16:7. How would you explain this to a child?

☐ We must pray with thanksgiving. Learn Colossians 4:2 by heart.

☐ We must be in earnest. Read James 5:7-18 and 1 Kings 18:41-46. The word fervent means "stretched out."

•PRAYING IT THROUGH•

Suggested Times

1. (On your own) Silently search within. Do you know of any sin? Confess it to the Lord. Think of any bad relationships in your life. Are you actively engaged in putting that right? Pray about it.

   5 minutes

2. (As a group) Let us remember who we come to when we pray. "Anyone who comes to Him must believe that He exists" (Heb. 11:6).
   > "We are coming to a King
   > Large petitions with you bring"
   ☐ Praise God for His person and His gracious giving of answers. Try to thank God for the way He has answered your requests.
   ☐ Pray for a friend who is a victim of his or her circumstances. Pray for his or her relationships, and that this person will have the courage to put them upright.

   10 minutes

3. (On your own) Imagine you are Elijah. Think about praying for:
   ☐ rain. What would stop you?
   ☐ fire from heaven.
   Now, think about something impossible you would like to ask God to do for you. Ask Him to do it as you think Elijah would ask Him to do it!

   5 minutes

•DIGGING DEEPER•

1. Read 1 Kings 17:7-16 and note the following observations:
Elijah's need:

Zarephath's and Sidon's locations:

The widow's probable nationality:

Her predicament:

God's command to Elijah:

God's command to the widow:

The widow's oath:

Elijah's instructions:

God's solution to Elijah's need:

God's solution to the widow's problem:

2. Why would God use a pagan to sustain His prophet? What other questions does this passage raise? List and try to answer as many as come to mind.

3. Read 1 Kings 17:17-24. Why are these two incidents recorded back to back?

4. What does verse 18 reveal that the widow recognized about God and about herself?

5. Review Elijah's prayer and examine the characteristics of his prayer.

6. What conditions for prayer did Elijah meet? What were several results of his prayer? What does this account teach you about prayer?

7. Why do you think this story was recorded?

8. Read 1 Kings 18:16-46. Why did Elijah accuse Ahab? (v. 18) Why did he accuse the people? (v. 21) What does the word *waver* mean? What does the people's silence suggest to you?

9. What did God think of Elijah's statement in verse 22? (cf. 19:10, 14, 15-18) Consider why God would answer an arrogant man's prayers.

10. What were Elijah's specific prayer requests? How did Elijah demonstrate faith at Mt. Carmel? How did this answered prayer affect the unbelievers present? The believers present?

11. Have you been guilty of "wavering" lately? If so, in what way?

12. What is the purpose behind most of your prayer requests? How do your prayers influence believers and unbelievers?

13. Review what you have learned from the Food For Thought and Digging Deeper sections of this chapter. Take time to prayerfully consider any conditions for prayer you may not be meeting and any hindrances to prayer you may be entertaining. Confess them. Then compose a prayer that you believe would be pleasing to God that is relative to your present circumstances.

For Further Study

1. Study the life of Elijah and complete your picture of this prophet. Notice his failures and successes. Discuss his personality strengths and weaknesses. Determine what he accomplished through and for God. What does his life teach you about prayer and about God?

2. Reread 1 Kings 17–18 several times, digesting the content. Ask a friend to then give you a content quiz of ten questions or so based on these two chapters.

•TOOL CHEST•
(A Suggested Optional Resource)

THE PROPHETS

In his two volume set, *The Prophets* (Harper and Row), Abraham J. Heschel introduces the reader to the caliber of character the prophets of the divided and nearly extinct kingdom maintained. Heschel acquaints us with the anguish of their lives, their critical message and call to justice, morality, and obedience to the Law.

These volumes help provide the student with a clearer understanding of the depth of God's love and breadth of His long-suffering. If you are seeking to grasp the tension and balance between God's sorrow and wrath toward His people's apathy and disobedience, *The Prophets* should help you with your pursuit. These and other tough questions are wrestled with to the reader's satisfaction.

6

Praying for Our Loved Ones

• FOOD FOR THOUGHT •

God loves our loved ones more than we do. It is through prayer that we come to this grand realization. If I do little praying, I will find myself subconsciously believing that even though God loves so-and-so, He cannot possibly love him as much as I do! This is understandable, I reason to myself. After all, I'm related to that person. He isn't. She's my wife; he's my son or daughter or boyfriend—therefore, I am in a better position to really care and understand. Prayer suddenly becomes a sort of protective layer I must use to shield them from an angry, judgmental God, who I believe is not very pleased with their lifestyle.

Communication with God about people involves our spending enough time with Him to enable us to understand how He really feels about those we love. If we will only talk it out in prayer and listen to His answers, we will make a remarkable discovery. We will find out that we are *not* more merciful, loving, and forgiving than God! We will discover we do not have to convince Him that our dear ones are not as bad as He thinks they are, and we do not have to remind Him of their good qualities. Neither need we explain the *reasons* for their disobedience. We do not need to try to "protect" them from His dealings with them at all, for we come to understand that His dealings with them are in *love*. An all-seeing, all-knowing, all-merciful *love*.

Let me illustrate the release this brings to our hearts. We find we can trust God with those we love. To trust is to find rest from concern, not because we prayed for them and saw Him jump to our commands, but because in prayer we have "seen" the heart of God toward them and can never doubt again that He loves them more than we do.

Stuart spent the first seven years of our married life traveling. This put much responsibility on my shoulders. I was to be mother and father to our three lively children. When he came home, it was difficult for me to suddenly relinquish that authority role to him. I felt he didn't know our kids as well as I did, simply because he was not around enough to know them. Therefore, I felt his dealings in judgment would not be according to knowledge. I felt I must avoid confrontation between each child and his father, and so I would anticipate trouble and always be hovering around to intervene on their behalf. I did not talk this out with my husband, and so the attitude remained.

When God graciously gave us time together as a family after 10 years of missionary work, I found the battle continued. Especially where our teenage daughter was concerned. *How could he possibly understand her?* I reasoned. She was a woman; she was extremely strong-willed; and I could see confrontations developing every 10 minutes. I exhausted myself "being around" to play the peacemaker. This went on until one day my husband sat me down and talked it out with me. He told me to get out of the way, because I was depriving him of a relationship with his own child. He too must be allowed to learn to know her. He was rightly hurt because I had not trusted him to handle her. The biggest thing I saw was his love for her. And even though I knew mistakes might be made, I also knew that love would be the key to judgment. The release from that responsibility was fantastic. I just physically removed myself from approaching situations and let them "meet." Meet they did, learn they did, and a beautiful relationship in love now exists between them. I trust my husband's dealings with our children, and the *rest* that results is a prize indeed.

This is what happens when you spend much time in prayer with God about those you love. If you identify with all this, you are in good company. Abraham felt the same struggle about Lot, as we see in Genesis 18:16-23. This passage of Scripture is not a grand example of Abraham's using prayer to change God's mind about his loved ones. It is a perfect example of God's changing Abraham's understanding of His mind. God's judgment was according to knowledge, tempered with grace, and demonstrated in loving concern and action on Lot's behalf. To "talk it out" is to spend time listening to the loving heartbeat of God toward those we care for most. Then we can make the best of discoveries: "God loves them *more* than I do!"

I have found myself pleading in prayer that God will not judge them! Now I realize that this is a pretty stupid way to pray. He has to be what He is—perfectly just. The judgment of God means man has value—his actions matter; therefore, he matters! A child who is never punished feels his actions have no consequences. Nobody cares what he does; therefore, he believes that what he does doesn't matter. There is no one in more trouble than the person who feels that he or she has no value. No, what we *are* matters to God, and what we *do* matters to God. He examines us closely, coming near to see if it's as bad as He thinks it is. *It is!* "Your life shouts to heaven for the judgment of God."

Now in prayer we come to believe that *whatever* the Judge of all the earth does *has* to be right, because *He is rightness*. When you have met with God as Abraham met with Him—Abraham, who stood on a hilltop and watched the judgment of God fall on a city full of people—and can say, "It must be right," then prayer has accomplished something.

As I studied the passage of Scripture concerning Abraham and Sodom, I realized that God didn't really *need* to get a closer look at the situation. He isn't shortsighted! It was for Abraham's sake that He came, so His friend might understand that He was willing, far beyond the requirements of mercy, to give Sodom yet another chance. Surely an angel visit would bring repentance! By the time Abraham had finished praying, he believed he could accept God's harsh dealings with his loved ones. Remember, as far as we know, Abraham never did know Lot was saved! All he saw was the smoke! Maybe it was just as well he probably didn't know. Better to think him dead than to learn the end of his degraded life, involving immorality with his own daughters (Gen. 19:30-38).

We need to ask God to prepare us through prayer for the things He knows will be happening, that we may believe He will deal with our loved ones in whatever way seems right to Him. That's hard—it may mean seeing judgment fall. But we will have discovered in prayer and through experience that there will *never* be judgment without mercy.

God loves those we love more than we do. He wishes to convey to us His care for those who matter most to us.

• TALKING IT OVER •

Suggested Times

---

1. READ AND DISCUSS.   *10 minutes*

Read Genesis 18:16-23. Discuss the following questions.

☐ What made God want to share His plans with Abraham? (vv. 17-19)

This passage raises serious questions. Reread verses 23-33.

☐ Was God right or "righteous" in bringing such terrible judgment?

☐ Whatever God does has to be right. Because He is righteous, He cannot do anything wrong. Do we believe this?

---

2. READ ALOUD AND DISCUSS.   *10 minutes*

Look up the following statements about the character of God and let the group read them aloud:

☐ Genesis 18:25

☐ Deuteronomy 7:9; 32:4

☐ Revelation 15:3; 16:7

Scripture claims God is always right in what He does. Sin must be judged; it is terrible. Therefore, God is right to judge it. Sin cost God His Son's life. Surely that demonstrates how seriously God sees sin.

☐ How do we know God was careful that He had His facts straight? (Gen. 18:21-22)

---

3. DISCUSS.   *10 minutes*

Can our prayers change God's mind about something He has decided? What are some relevant statements in these passages:

☐ Isaiah 40:12-31

☐ Romans 11:33-34

☐ 1 Corinthians 2:16

Discuss what Abraham learned about God through his experience (Gen. 18:16-33).

☐ About His fairness (v. 21)

☐ About His grace (v. 26)

☐ About speaking to a Holy God (vv. 27, 30, 32)

☐ About God's generosity (v. 32)

•PRAYING IT THROUGH•

Suggested Times

---

1. (On your own) Make a list of all your loved ones. Decide if you believe God loves them more than you do. Then write a short letter to God telling Him what you feel about them and also what you have learned through the story of Abraham about what He feels for them.

5 minutes

---

2. (In twos) Share one concern you have for a loved one with your partner. Pray for that person.

5 minutes

---

3. (As a group) Read Psalm 23. Then pray through the psalm for your loved ones. For example, "Lord, I pray for _____, may he come to know You as his personal Shepherd."

5 minutes

---

4. (As a group) Be still and think about God and His love. Imagine Him smiling at the people you love—praying for them—working for their good. Praise Him for that.

5 minutes

•DIGGING DEEPER•

Praying for Believing Loved Ones

1. Read Colossians 1:9-14. Isolate Paul's specific prayer request for his "holy and faithful brothers in Christ" (v. 2).

   What does this passage teach us about the frequency of our prayers?

2. Define spiritual wisdom and understanding.

   What changes do you suspect would occur in your loved one if he/she were "fill(ed) . . . with the knowledge of His will"?

3. Paul mentions a specific aim for his prayer. What is that aim? (cf. 2 Cor. 5:9)

   Think honestly about your recent prayers for a dear one. What has been the goal of your prayer?

4. Several effects of Paul's specific prayer request are elaborated on in verses 10-12. What are they?

What do the effects "great endurance and patience" imply?

5. Is there any content absent from Paul's prayer that you might expect to find?

6. What does the verb *rescued* in verse 14 suggest to you about the Father?

Have you been guilty lately of playing the rescuer for a loved one? Ask your Father to show you how to allow Him to be the rescuer instead. Record your prayer in the space provided.

Praying for Unbelieving Loved Ones
7. Read Numbers 14:10-35. Pinpoint Moses' prayer requests.

8. What was God willing to do in this situation? What was He unwilling to do?

9. Imagine you are Moses. Consider what you would have learned from this prayer experience.

10. How does this passage correspond with what Paul wrote about God being a rescuer? (cf. Ex. 16:1-8; 17:1-7; 19:3-8; 32:9-14; 34:8-14)

11. From your study, list the principles we can be assured of when we pray for an unbelieving loved one.

    Record an appropriate prayer for someone you have been praying for who falls under this category.

For Further Study
1. Read 1 Peter 2:13-25 and decide how you might pray for a loved one who is in the midst of adversity.
2. Read Philippians 4:10-13 and determine how you might pray for a loved one who is in the midst of prosperity.

•TOOL CHEST•
(A Suggested Optional Resource)

IN HIS STEPS

In His Steps (Brownlow) by Charles M. Sheldon is one of those "musts" for your personal book collection. It seeks to answer the questions: What is true Christian discipleship? How do we live out the life of Christ in our daily work, home, and activities? What does it look like to follow in the steps of the Lord Jesus in a world of social evils and injustices? The reader is introduced in this novel to a pastor and a few members of his flock who pledge themselves for one year to live by the guiding principle, "What would Jesus do?" and to implement their conclusions no matter what the personal cost. *In His Steps* makes for very challenging and thought-provoking reading.

7
Praying for Ourselves

•FOOD FOR THOUGHT•

"Pray for me, Mum." Pete bounced off the bottom step and onto the sidewalk as he issued his directive. He was on his way to start another school year with new hopes and dreams, new incentives, new goals.

"Sure, Pete," I replied. "What for?" His answer took me aback.

"I want first-chair clarinet," he announced.

"But, Pete," I remonstrated, "I can't pray *that* for you—you haven't practiced in three months!"

"Well," he replied, looking mildly perturbed, "if I'd practiced, I wouldn't need *you* to pray!" I decided it was time to talk to Pete about prayer!

Some of you reading these pages want first-chair Christian. That's a great and noble goal. I would encourage you in your eagerness for the necessary holiness of life that sets you apart from the defeated fifty-first-chair disciple! But you can't have first-chair Christian overnight; just as you can't have first-chair clarinet without practicing for three months. That's the word—*practice!* It means going at a difficult set of circumstances from every possible way until you have mastered it. First-chair clarinet conjures up certain words to my mind—words like *time, effort, discipline, stickability, determination*, and, above all, *instruction from a master!* First-chair Christian brings to mind similar ideas.

Many people believe prayer is a magic wand; they expect to wave it to and fro in God's face and be changed from Cinderella into the princess. All they have to do is pray and God will give them the things they don't deserve.

Now God always *does* give us things we don't deserve, for if He gave us what we *do* deserve, we would all be crucified! But prayer, someone has said, is simply the "debating chamber of the soul." Here a subject is brought up for debate by the Master, and a frank and open discussion of all aspects is intended to take place. The subject is chosen carefully by God. Let us return to our analogy of master musician and pupil. God is not interested in producing by magic a finished symphony. He intends the pupil's character to be "finished" as he works on the Master's instructions and practices faithfully whatever skills are set for the lesson of the day.

The Master instructs, and we practice. He chooses the piece of music. We play it. Instead of trying to use prayer as a briefing time for the Almighty, telling Him to "magic up" some nice conclusions to a sticky situation we have brought upon ourselves, prayer should be a briefing time for *us* to hear how we can bring about our own conclusions! Prayer isn't telling God to practice something, but it is Him giving us *our* homework! If we give Him half a chance to get us alone regularly, He will change *us* and work with us that we may become the answer to our own prayers. Prayer is our opportunity to receive instruction that may require *action* on our part.

Now, to recapitulate: You remember praise gives us a vision of God, which leads to a vision of self and a vision of others, and then demands availability for action! "Here am I, send me" is the grand conclusion of praise (Isa. 6:8). Sometimes our service of inadequacy is so overwhelming that we become overawed at the command received in prayer, and so we protest instead of yield. Like Moses we say, "Here I am, send Aaron!" Or, like Jonah, we don't say anything at all.

Do you remember the story of Jonah? He was in prayer about the Assyrian people. They had been harassing Israel; and Jonah, a patriotic, nationalistic-minded Jew, was busy feeding the hatred in his heart toward his country's enemies. I'm sure he was demanding that Jehovah wipe them off the face of the earth. Instead, God told him to go and preach to them that He might have a chance to forgive! This way Jonah would become the answer to his own prayer. Nineveh would repent and get off Israel's back. You see, God is utterly committed to answering our prayers *His* way! But His way was not a way Jonah was ready to accept. Jonah's quiet time came to an abrupt halt. There was no way prayer could continue when the presence of the Lord meant obeying a command like that!

It is in prayer that we will find the will of God, but to find God's will is not necessarily to find ourselves willing to *do* it. If we continue in prayer, debating the issue until we can say as Jesus did, "Nevertheless *not* My will but Thine be done" (Luke 22:42), then the purpose of prayer is accomplished; but if we say instead, "Not Thy will, but *mine* be done," we have no alternative but to do as Jonah did and "flee from the presence of the Lord." What is your Nineveh? What are you running away from as fast as you can go?

What I love about the attitude of God toward Jonah is the unavoidable inference in the story of God's great concern for His prejudiced prophet! Even though Nineveh must be given a chance to repent—for God is an internationalist and longs that *all* should be saved—His concern was also for the blessings of His angry, resentful servant! God was about to manifest His power in many miraculous events in these chapters, but the greatest miracle was to be the changed heart and attitude of Jonah. He needed to repent as well as Nineveh, and God intended to give him that opportunity.

When we pray for ourselves, our petitions usually center around what we think we need or what we are sure so-and-so needs. God sees needs in our lives that are far more urgent than those we have written on our heavenly supermarket list and daily present to our "Need-Meeter" in the sky. Our need for changed attitudes, a new acceptance of someone we have been rejecting, our need to be "cut down to size"—these are not things we pray for too readily. On the other hand, we do find we can pray these things for other people!

Do you, for example, find yourself asking God to thoroughly humble you, or to give you the grand opportunity to spend a lot of time with the very person you hate? Do you hear yourself asking God to allow you to make an absolute fool of yourself for Christ's sake?

When God told Jonah to go to Nineveh, it was not unrelated to Jonah's passionate request for his beleaguered country. It was to be the beginning of the answer to his prayer. But, oh, the "Much more" of God. He intended not only to meet Nineveh's and Israel's needs, but Jonah's need as well. *And,* incidentally, God's need would be met as He saw the results of the travail of His soul and would be satisfied. God was committed to making Jonah like His Son. God wanted him to learn to love what he had every right to hate, and to know the blessings that come to those who love their enemies.

I remember the day I realized God was committed to straightening me out. "The crooked roads shall become straight" (Luke 3:5). The Bible says there are not crooked Christians allowed in God's camp! He is committed to making a highway for Himself through my life, and that means leveling the hills of pride and prejudice.

Even when I am not committed to letting Him straighten my crooked parts, my stubbornness, and my dislike of others who are not as I am, He is still committed to doing it. He overtakes me in my headlong plunge away from those "straightening" circumstances . . . just as He did with Jonah.

Jonah found it was useless to try to run away from God's instructions, because God has longer legs! Jonah had a truly "in-depth" experience over the whole thing!

Yes, God was indeed committed to making Jonah like His Son, just as He is committed to making us like Christ too. We will need to be praying for ourselves to that end.

But there is one main reason we shall find it terribly difficult to pray for ourselves. Not only are we ourselves often our own worst enemies where prayer is concerned—the great enemy of our prayer life is Satan himself. It is he we so often battle when we attempt to pray. Prayer is the God-given atomic weapon against evil powers that Satan must prevent being used at all costs. Remember,

> Satan trembles when he sees,
> The weakest saint upon his knees.

The source of my authority is God who worked with a mighty power (Eph. 1:19). If I doubt how powerful He is, I can simply think of the demonstration of that power when God raised Christ from the dead! Someone has said, "The devil laughed at the cross, but stopped laughing at the Resurrection." In God I can challenge the evil authority that holds fast the people who are without Christ, without hope, and without God on this earth.

Like a traffic director in the midst of a traffic jam, I am invested with the authority of the government. I represent it, even though in my small person I am so much "less" than the cars I direct. When I raise my hand, I can confront and stop the traffic.

This power that enables me to stand in front of Satan "in Christ" has much to do with the wrestling of prayer. There is an unseen battle going on before I even get in on the act. We have almost no idea what is happening a hidden sense away. You remember Elisha prayed that God would open his servant's eyes to see the unseen forces surrounding and protecting them, and God did just that for the discouraged and frightened servant.

He would do that for us as well. There are good spirits constantly working on our behalf in the heavenly places, just as surely as there are evil forces working against us and against those for whom we are praying.

Behind the mighty rulers of our world stand evil or good angels influencing them.

Not only do we have to contend with direct attacks of the evil one against us, but we must be aware that we enter a spiritual battlefield whenever we simply drop to our knees and say, "Our Father. . . ."

Like Moses, we have to learn that the "I Am" has sent us to stand before Pharaoh and demand with all of heaven's authority behind us that he let the people go! Satan, who stood behind that earthly Pharaoh, might tighten his grip upon the people as soon as we begin to pray, but if we rebuke him in the name of the Lord, because of our position in Christ, he will have no alternative but to give them up. It is then up to the people in bondage to exercise their free will and leave! The choice is theirs. God will not, and we must not, violate their right to choose. But praying "back" the forces of evil, while that choice is made, is a wrestling pastime that is the believer's privilege, yea, even his responsibility . . . that the air might be cleared around those we pray for so that God's voice may be clearly heard!

•TALKING IT OVER•

1. READ AND DISCUSS.   *10 minutes*
   Read Jonah 2, then discuss the following ques-
   tions:
   ☐ Why did Jonah start praying again? (vv. 2, 7)
   ☐ How can we make sure this does not become a
   pattern of our prayer lives?
   ☐ What immediate assurances did Jonah receive?
   (v. 2)
   ☐ How did the rebellious prophet bring himself
   back into touch with God? (v. 4) Were his
   mind, emotions, or will involved?
   ☐ Affliction sharpens all our remembrances. Just
   what did Jonah remember? (v. 9)
   ☐ God assures us of His control over the events of
   our lives (v. 10). Quickly examine Romans
   8:28, 35-39, and Psalm 23. Spend a few minutes praying about what you have learned.
   What vows have you forgotten? Can you even
   begin to praise God for the whale?
   ☐ Share an experience you have had of rebellion
   against God's revealed will. Tell the group
   about the "whale" God used to bring you back!

2. READ, LIST, AND DISCUSS.   *10 minutes*
   Read Ephesians 6:12 and make a list of the un-
   seen powers we wrestle against. Then read Ephe-
   sians 1:18-23 and answer these questions:
   ☐ Where is Christ now? (v. 20)
   ☐ What is His position above? (v. 21)
   ☐ What is His relationship to the church? (v. 22)
   ☐ Am I a part of His body? (v. 23; 1 Corinthians
   12:12-14)
   ☐ What is my position in Christ in relation to the
   authorities and unseen wicked powers? (v. 22;
   Ephesians 1:3)

3. READ AND DISCUSS.   *10 minutes*
   Read Daniel 10:1-9 on your own or in pairs. For
   three full weeks Daniel had been praying and

fasting, experiencing a great spirit of heaviness. He received a vision of God (vv. 5-6) which led to a sense of his own unworthiness. We have already talked about the effect a vision of God has on a man in our first study, and here we see a similar effect on Daniel (vv. 8-9). Another angel appears and touches Daniel, strengthening him and commanding him to stand upright. He reminds him how greatly God loves him and reassures him that the Father has seen his right attitude of heart, heard his prayer, and has immediately dispatched His angel emissary with the answer (v. 12). Then why three weeks' delay?

•PRAYING IT THROUGH•

Suggested Times

1. (As a group) Think about whether you have ever prayed prayers similar to my son Pete's. What stopped you? Spend a few moments right now in quiet contemplation and answer the question, What is my Ninevah? If you can, talk to God about it.

5 minutes

2. (In twos) Remind yourselves of Jonah's prayer in Jonah 2.
   ☐ What *one* thing does this chapter teach you about your own prayer life? Pray about it.
   ☐ Spend a little time "wrestling" over some matter of concern, some spiritual battle. Claim Christ's authority over Satan concerning this. Praise Him for the victory He has won for you because of His death and resurrection.

5 minutes

3. Pray about people you know in the leadership of your church who are like Daniel—experiencing a spirit of heaviness. Make a list of their names.

5 minutes

4. Pray for yourself that God will strengthen you as He strengthened Daniel.

5 minutes

•DIGGING DEEPER•

Paul's prayers are good models of how we ought to pray for ourselves. As we study one of them, compare your personal prayer requests with his.

1. Read Philippians 1:9-11. Then review the surrounding context. What attitude do Paul's petitions naturally flow from? What does this teach you about prayer?

2. Rewrite in your own words Paul's specific request.

   By what standard is our love to be measured?

3. Are there any clues in the passage to help you define "knowledge and depth of insight"?

   How do commentators define these terms and why?

   Now describe how our increasing love is to be characterized. Give a practical example.

4. Consider what we learned from the life of Jonah in the Food For Thought section of this chapter. What might you anticipate to be the process you would undergo to have this prayer answered? Please be specific and personal in your reply.

5. "To be able to discern what is best" means deciding between what two options?

6. Think of a circumstance in which you are unsure of what is best. According to Paul's prayer, how can you come to the right conclusion?

7. How does "until the day of Christ" function in this passage? Why is it here, and what is its purpose?

8. To be "filled with the fruit of righteousness" has at least two possible interpretations. Using Bible resources, explain the various meanings, stating which you prefer and why.

9. What is the ultimate goal of this prayer and of what is it reminiscent?

10. Take time now to ask God how you ought to be praying for yourself. After a period of quiet reflection, list below what you believe He has said to you.

11. Review your study on prayer from each chapter of this book. What lessons and principles have you learned regarding prayer?

For Further Study
1. Read Ephesians 1:15-23. Identify Paul's requests and corresponding effects of each. What does the metaphor "eyes of the heart" describe? Define "the hope to which He has called you." How would such assurance influence your daily life, struggles, and outlook? How would the reality of "the riches of His glorious inheritance" and "His incomparably great power for us" in your life make a difference?
2. Compare Paul's prayer in Philippians 1:9-11 with Ephesians 1:15-23. What are the similarities? Where was Paul located when he wrote each of these prayers? In light of this, what is unusual about his requests? What does this teach you?

•TOOL CHEST•
(A Suggested Optional Resource)

BOOKS ON PRAYER

You will want to build into your library a section on prayer books, helps, and Bible studies. These have been written to enhance the Christian's prayer life, not replace it. Such tools could be used to supplement your daily quiet time with the Lord or to study as a group. Check your local bookstore, church, or pastor's library for some of the following classic books on prayer.

Adventures In Prayer by Catherine Marshall (Ballantine)
Answers To Prayer by Charles G. Finney (Bethany)
Believer's School of Prayer by Andrew Murray (Bethany)
Believer's Secret of Waiting On God by Andrew Murray (Bethany)
Communicating Love Through Prayer by Rosalind Rinker (Revell)
Daring To Draw Near by John White (InterVarsity)
Discovering How To Pray by Hope MacDonald (Zondervan)
Effective Prayer by R.C. Sproul (Tyndale)
George Mueller: Man of Faith by Basil Miller (Bethany)
God Listens by Samuel Chadwick (Back to the Bible)
The God Who Hears by W. Bingham Hunter (InterVarsity)
Handle With Prayer by Charles Stanley (Victor)
Hearing God by Peter Lord (Baker)
How I Know God Answers Prayer by Rosalind Goforth (Bethel)
How To Pray by R.A. Torrey (Moody)
Jesus' Pattern of Prayer by John MacArthur (Moody)
The Joy Of Listening To God by Joyce Huggett (InterVarsity)
Layman Looks At The Lord's Prayer by Phillip Keller (Moody)
No Easy Road by Dick Eastman (Baker)
Power of Positive Praying by John Bisagno (Zondervan)
Practicing His Presence by Brother Lawrence (Christian Books Publishing House)
Prayer by O. Hallesby (Augsburg)
Prayer—Conversing With God by Rosalind Rinker (Revell)
Praying For One Another by Gene Getz (Victor)
Praying Together by Charlie Shedd and Martha Shedd (Zondervan)
Principles Of Prayer by Charles G. Finney (Bethany)
Sense and Nonsense About Prayer by Lehman Strauss (Moody)
Too Busy Not To Pray by Bill Hybels (InterVarsity)
What Happens When Women Pray by Evelyn Christenson (Victor)

8

More Exciting Prayer Meetings

•FOOD FOR THOUGHT•

Some of the most boring times of my Christian life have been spent in church prayer meetings. Some of the funniest times of my Christian life have been spent in church prayer meetings. And some of the most blessed times. What makes the difference? What ingredients are needed to turn a prayer meeting from a bane into a blessing?

First of all, we have to learn to deal with *Mrs. Mumbler.* Off she goes, mumbling and bumbling. Her head is down, and her words are shooting straight into the shag carpet. All of us are nearly falling off our chairs in an effort to hear. It wouldn't be so bad, but she goes on and on; and then just when there's a pause and someone thinks it's all over, off she goes again, to the great embarrassment of the unintentional interrupter.

There is only one way out of this. As leader of the group, tell everyone (looking straight at Mrs. Mumbler) that we will keep our heads up to pray, speak loud enough for all to hear, and if anyone prays too softly, you will stop the person praying and ask for more volume.

Next, you may have a *Mr. Got-to-tell-you-all-I-know* in your group. This is a man who can't wait to impart his scriptural knowledge to the people in the prayer meeting. The Scripture phrases flow on and on, as we trace the journeys of the Children of Israel through the wilderness into the Promised Land, listen to the various prophets (were there really that many?) thunder their exhortations, and finish up with a quick survey of New Testament theology. When he eventually stops, everyone is so stunned there is a loud silence which he mistakes for appreciation!

Then there is *Miss Steal-everything-there-is-to-pray-about-before-you-get-a-turn*. This young lady really *is* a menace. You carefully enumerate the prayer requests. You can see one or two eager, but shy, young people who have come for the first time, and you want to give them plenty of items to choose from. Then Miss Steal-everything starts. She uses up every item on the list and ends with a triumphant, "So, Lord, continue with us as we pray on." *Little Miss Frightened-out-of-her-mind* sitting next to her is, of course, left with absolutely nothing to say. She has sat there in horror as item after item was used up, her mind frantically trying to think of some other petition. That is the way to make sure she never comes back again! As leader, you *must* make sure you ask the group to pray for only one or two requests at the most.

Then you have *Mrs. Can't-wait-to-tell-you-all-the-juicy-gossip-I-can't-tell-you-with-my-eyes-open!* This is an obnoxious lady who uses the public prayer meeting to pass on juicy news—all under the disguise of praying for poor so-and-so. "Help Mrs. H. to know she must not have an affair with a married man now that she's a Christian," she prays in a hushed, sad monotone.

Now this *has* to be stopped, and I suggest that the leader tell the group no names or situations must be revealed unless the item to be prayed about is common knowledge. The public prayer meeting was never intended to be a place to reveal private scandals.

Then there is *Mr. Correct-your-prayer*. He is the one who listens to a "starter prayer" and feels it his duty to catch the prayer in midair, sort it out, and deliver it as he knows it was intended to the Almighty! He is really doing the Holy Spirit's job, which is to sort out all our prayers and present the essence of them before the Father.

What do you do with the noisy pray-ers? Now, *amen* and *hallelujah* are scripturally proper in such places as a praise meeting, but what is important is consideration of others in the group, who may be disturbed by the noisiness of the amens. Furthermore, I have been in prayer meetings when amen—which means "so be it"—was added in ridiculous fashion to all sorts of statements. We must intelligently articulate our "so-be-its" at the right times only if they will edify and unify the group, and if they do not cause uneasiness or division.

"How good and how pleasant it is for brethren to dwell together in unity" (Ps. 133:1). The leader should pray about all these problems, be brave enough to approach the offenders in love and talk with them, and also plan a variety of prayer meetings using different formats to encourage new prayers and curtail long ones. A planned format is helpful to correct many of these problems.

As an exercise in our groups as we studied corporate prayer, the members worked out a planned format of a prayer meeting. Some examples appear later in this chapter, many of which we have used in our own prayer times. You may like to use one or more of them in yours. We put people into pairs to work out a thirty-minute prayer time. Maybe you can put some formats together too. You could collect them, place them in a file, and then recruit leaders who would use. them in your church.

Corporate Prayer
Work together answering the questions and discussing the gathered information.

What the Bible Says
1. What is the minimum size for a corporate prayer meeting? (Matt. 18:19-20)
2. What is the maximum size? (Acts 2:41-42; Rev. 19:1-6)
3. When we come together, the atmosphere should be one of: confusion, variety, peace, criticism, edification, order, frenzy, decency, noise, unity. Read 1 Cor. 14:26, 33, 40 and circle the right words.
4. Read the account of Peter's miraculous release from prison in Acts 12:5-17. Discuss the following questions:
   ☐ How hard was the church praying? (v. 5)
   ☐ What effect was their prayer having on Peter in prison? (v. 6)
   ☐ How did he know where the church would be? (v. 12)
   ☐ Do you think Rhoda was expecting Peter? (vv. 14-15)
   ☐ Was the church expecting an answer to their prayers? (vv. 15-16)
   ☐ What does this story remind us about corporate prayer on behalf of our brothers and sisters in prison for their faith?
   ☐ What defects did this particular corporate prayer meeting appear to have?
   ☐ What good things were happening as a result of this prayer meeting?

Application
1. Make a list of the do's and don'ts to be observed in a prayer meeting.
2. Working in pairs, plan a half-hour prayer meeting for your church or group. Use all the ideas you have learned about.

3. Go to your pastor and ask if you can help with the prayer meeting. (Pick him up after he has fainted with shock and assure him you mean it.) After all, you really have no alternative but to obey the commandment of the Lord, who said, "When you pray, say. . . ."

How to Pray for the Church

To inform group members of our class about the needs of the church, we invited several officers of our church to come and share their needs with the people. Dividing the large group into smaller units, we put an officer with each group for fifteen minutes. For five minutes they shared and for five minutes the group asked questions. For the last five minutes they prayed about those requests. We had a tremendous response to this. The officers were delighted, and the group members were thrilled the very next week to hear about the answers to their intercessions.

As an example, our caretaker had been asked to share his problems, and he communicated the need for a student helper to clean the church building in the evenings. They had tried for weeks to find one but had not been successful. The little groups prayed, and next week the caretaker returned to ask if he could share the results. *Two* students had applied for the job that very week, and they had employed the one who appeared more suitable!

Other people you could invite to share could be:

Head of nursery	Sunday School superintendent
Caretaker	Youth leader
A deacon or elder	Member of church finance committee
Your pastor	Sound-system technician
A hospital visitor	Tape ministry representative
Office personnel	Missions committee representative

If you are endeavoring to do this study on your own, you can personally approach each one and become fully informed as to your church's prayer needs. You could also invite them to the church prayer meeting to explain their prayer needs. Have one of these persons sit in each group as they discuss the various Scriptures. Then have the group pray specifically for that person.

1. **Caretaker** This person is responsible for the protection and maintenance of a great variety of things in the church (2 Kings

23:4; 1 Chron. 9:26-33; Ps. 121:3-4). His qualities are to be:
□
□
□

2. **Deacon or Elder** These men are to "serve tables" and "teach" if needed (1 Tim. 3:1-13; Acts 6:1-6). Their character is to be:
□
□
□
□
□
□

3. **Pastor** The pastor is to possess the qualities of a deacon or elder as well as those of a shepherd. What are the qualities of a shepherd? (Ps. 23)
□
□
□
□
□
□

4. **Missions Committee** This busy and functional arm of the church is an extension over the world in a material as well as spiritual way. They need (Luke 22:32; John 4:35-36; Eph. 6:19; Col. 4:3):
□
□
□

5. **Youth worker** Timothy is a living example of youth in the Bible. His spiritual father, Paul, encouraged him and probably prayed for him in these areas. List as many as you can find from 1 Timothy 1:18-19 and 2:11-16:
□
□
□
□
□

6. **Music Committee** Music is a means of worship, praise, and expressing our emotions to the Lord. We are to sing with (1 Cor. 14:15):
□
□

Therefore, we should pray _____ and
_____ for our music committee.

The Prayer Calendar/Card File
Roselyn Aronson, Children's Pastor at Elmbrook Church, brought a helpful tool along to share with us—the prayer calendar/card file. The discovery of this simple tool has been helpful to me in maintaining an exciting, consistent prayer life. When mixed with discipline and a desire to be taught by the Holy Spirit, it enables freedom and flexibility to permeate a prayer calendar.

The tangible articles necessary to begin are a pack of 3 x 5 cards, a card file, and a pen. The operative tool will consist of cards with individual prayer reminders appropriately filed on a daily or weekly basis. This tool will help us in our personal prayer life, but one also may be kept at the prayer meeting for the use of the fellowship.

In order to establish a series of cards distinctive to yourself, begin by asking the Holy Spirit to make you sensitive to the needs of which He would have you aware. As people and/or ideas come to mind, start a card by marking an appropriate heading and noting the date and thought. For example, the lifestyle of my friend, John, who is not a Christian, has been abruptly affected by the discovery of metastatic cancer. The burden on my heart is that he come to know the Lord Jesus. My card for him begins:

John	
9/2 Crisis	Salvation

Remember that the cards are tools, not burdens; keep them simple. They are personal between you and God; no one else needs to understand them.

When you have established a card for each need of which you are aware, sort them into daily and weekly categories according to urgency and depth of need.

Try to remember that it is more effective to pray fervently once a week than to read off a list of names daily. Cards can be transferred from weekly to daily or vice versa as needs change. Keep a supply of blank cards; new needs will appear.

Make some dividers for your card file with headings DAILY, MONDAY, TUESDAY, etc. Then each day as you pray, you will consider the pack of daily cards and the pack of weekly cards for that day. The card will serve as a reminder and will also give opportunity to keep a progress record. As you discuss with God, on an ongoing basis, the specific need of which the card' reminds you, you will receive new insight and observe changes which will be too exciting not to record. A new date is then noted with a new entry.

One of my most precious cards records for me my sister's salvation experience. The entries reveal my concern for her in relationships with others and her need for a relationship with the Lord Jesus Christ.

Name
7/10 need for Christian friend. 8/5 _____ _____
8/26 _____ 10/1 moved in with Christian roommate!!
10/1 _____ 10/15 Conviction. 10/15 Commitment!!!!
10/24 _____. etc.

As you develop your prayer file, you will want to make adaptations that will effectually gear this tool to your personal needs. You may want to develop a "praise card" and observe the changing character of your praise to God as you grow in your relationship with Him. You may want to develop a very secret "repent card" and observe your progressive awareness of areas of darkness in your life as you continue to expose yourself more and more to His light. You may want to record scriptural promises or prayer models specific to your situation. Be creative!

Regardless of individual adaptations, however, a common privilege will be enjoyed. Namely, the opportunity to flip through your old cards from time to time and reflect on the miracles!

Some Sample Formats for Prayer Meetings
These were put together by groups in our prayer class. Your class can do this too!

Format Number One
1. Leader: Begin group session with a short prayer for guidance and open hearts.

☐ Have a silent prayer and meditation time, fixing minds and thoughts on God.

☐ Explain a simple definition of prayer and locate several areas in Scripture where prayer is mentioned.

☐ Mention different types of prayer: praise, repentance, asking for others, asking for self.

2. General prayertime—following the above format.
3. Ask the group to cite conditions for prayer as stated in the Bible.
4. Share personal answers to prayer.

Format Number Two: Praise, Petitions, Prayer
1. First 10 minutes: a song of praise and thank-you testimonies.
2. Next 10 minutes: prayer requests for missionaries, for the church, and for things mentioned by those present.
3. Last 10 minutes: fervent prayer by each one present for the things mentioned and other personal problems.

Format Number Three
1. Begin with a few minutes of fellowship:
   ☐ Praise song
   ☐ Sharing from personal lives
2. Organize prayer requests and assign them to individuals.
3. Pray, using a psalm to praise God. Each member of the group can say a verse out loud.
4. In pairs, pray for requests shared.
5. Pray with prayer partner about your own personal requests.
6. Close with sentence prayers of thanksgiving.

Format Number Four: For Health of the Church Fellowship
Jesus calls us to prayer: Read Matthew 11:28-30.
Praise: Read Psalm 111:1-3.
Prayer for guidance: Read Psalm 16:7-8; 43:5; 30:21. Others may add their own prayers.
Making things right: Read John 15:12-13; Romans 12:14-21; and James 5:16. Others may add their own prayers for members of the body of Christ and for specific needs.
Close: Give thanks and prayers of thanksgiving.

Format Number Five (1 hour)
1. Call to order (5 minutes):
   ☐ Leader opens with prayer.
   ☐ Group has silent prayer, committing time to Christ and repent-

ing for loss of fellowship with Christ
☐ Leader closes with prayer.
2. Praise and thank God (20 minutes):
☐ For what He has done (Gen. 1:26-30).
☐ For what He will do (Rev. 22:1-5).
☐ For giving you a chance to talk with Him (Matt. 27:51; Mark 15:38; Heb. 4:14-16).
3. Pray for God's will to be done by the pastoral staff (10 minutes):
☐ That God will strengthen them in Spirit; in dedication and knowledge; in physical strength and health.
☐ For staff families.
4. Pray for fellowship (10 minutes):
☐ To strengthen tolerance of each other and commitment to Christ.
☐ For commitment to help the church recognize their spiritual gifts and commit those gifts to the church.
5. Pray for your needs (15 minutes):
☐ Physical and spiritual.
☐ Other personal prayer requests.

Format Number Six: "Praise" Prayer Meeting Schedule
1. Leader: Greeting
         Read psalm of praise
2. Split up into groups of four.
3. Quiet time for personal repentance.
4. Share what God is doing in individual lives and proceed to praise God in prayer.
5. Open to the Book of Psalms and share verses of praise and glory to God.
6. Large group together for time of praising God for who He is, what He does, His qualities.
7. Time of fellowship.

Format Number Seven (1 hour)
1. Leader begins in prayer, using the pattern of prayer:
☐ Praise
☐ Repentance
☐ Asking for others
☐ Asking for yourself
2. Leader points out that any passage of Scripture may be prayed through with this pattern of prayer. Divide into small groups and read Psalm 1 through twice—once out loud, once in silence.

☐ Share all things you can praise God for (vv. 1-3, 6). Then pray.
☐ Can you find anything to repent about? (vv. 1-3) Pray.
☐ Ask for others as this passage applies to them (vv. 1-6). Pray.
☐ Ask for self. Discuss your needs that have been brought to mind by this passage. Pray.

3. Leader reminds group that there are conditions to prayer, and if negative conditions prevail in your life, prayer will remain unanswered and unrewarding. *Sin in your tent affects the whole congregation!* (Josh. 7:1-26) As time permits, choose a favorite passage of Scripture and pray through it with the "pattern for prayer."

Format Number Eight (30 minutes)

Ground Rules
1. Have hosts and hostesses make everyone feel welcome as they arrive.
2. Be informal, and keep people close together, not scattered throughout the house, auditorium, etc.
3. Have a leader in each small group who will be able to pray and make others feel relaxed and at ease enough to pray.
4. Have a definite starting time. Don't get carried away chatting.

Organization
1. Leader opens meeting for a time of sharing answered prayers, ways God is working, etc.
2. Sing. Leader leads a prayer of thanksgiving and opens it up for prayer requests.
3. Split into small groups of 3-5 people. Divide prayer requests among groups.
4. Set aside time for sharing of more individual prayer requests.
5. Pray with a time limit.
6. Close with a time of fellowship and plans for the next meeting.

Format Number Nine
1. Choose a topic such as world affairs.
2. Leader opens with prayer.
3. Participants discuss different events from newspaper articles, broadcasts, etc.
4. Break up into groups of two or three to pray, each taking a specific subject mentioned.
5. Either come back to the large group or stay in small groups for concluding prayer time.

Format Number Ten
1. Leader could open with:
   ☐ Singing.
   ☐ Sharing of what God's been doing.
   ☐ Spontaneous Scripture reading.
2. Prayer:
   ☐ Praise.
   ☐ Bless the needy.
   ☐ Pray for our enemies and those we have trouble loving.
   ☐ People in authority over us.
   ☐ Increased faith.
   ☐ Availability to God for His will.
3. End by splitting into pairs, sharing one personal need or request with each other, and committing yourself to pray for that person all week.

Collecting Prayers
Another way of encouraging prayer is to suggest the group collect other people's prayers and make them their own. Our class enjoyed doing this. Here are a few examples they brought in. We added them to our file to be used if anyone so desired.

> "O Lord, Almighty God of our fathers, Abraham, Isaac, and Jacob, and of their righteous seed; who hast made heaven and earth, with all the ornament thereof; who hast bound the sea by the word of thy commandment; who hast shut up the deep, and sealed it by thy terrible and glorious name . . . My transgressions are multiplied, and I am not worthy to behold and see the height of heaven for the multitude of mine iniquities. I am bowed down with many iron bands, that I cannot lift up mine head, neither have any release: for I have provoked thy wrath, and done evil before thee: I did not thy will, neither kept I thy commandments: I have set up abominations, and have multiplied offenses. Now therefore I bow the knee of mine heart, beseeching thee of grace."

> Manasseh, King of Judah,
> when he was being held
> captive in Babylon

O to grace how great a debtor
Daily I'm constrained to be;

Let that grace now, like a fetter,
  Bind my wandering heart to thee.
Prone to wander, Lord, I feel it,
  Prone to leave the God I love—
Take my heart, O take and seal it,
  Seal it for thy courts above!

from the hymn "Come, Thou Fount of Every Blessing"
written by Robert Robinson, 1758

Slow Me Down

Slow me down, Lord, I'm going too fast;
I can't see my brother when he's walking past.
I miss a lot of good things day by day.
I don't know a blessing when it comes my way.
Slow me down, Lord; I want to see more of the things
That are good for me.
A little less of me and a little more of You.
I want the heavenly atmosphere to trickle through.
Let me help a brother when the going's rough;
When folks work together, it ain't so tough.
Slow me down, Lord, so I can talk with some of Your angels.
Slow me down to a walk.

Unknown

"Father, I want to know Thee, but my coward heart fears to give up its toys. I cannot part with them without inward bleeding, and I do not try to hide from Thee the terror of the parting. I come trembling, but I do come. Please root from my heart all those things which I have cherished so long, and which have become a very part of my living self, so that Thou mayest enter and dwell there without a rival. Then shalt Thou make the place of Thy feet glorious. Then shall my heart have not need of the sun to shine in it, for Thyself wilt be the light of it, and there shall be no night there."

A.W. Tozer
The Pursuit of God

Answer to Prayer

We ask for strength and God gives—
us difficulties to make us strong.

We pray for wisdom and God sends—
us problems,
The solution of which develops wisdom.

We plead for prosperity and God gives—
us brain and brawn to work.

We plead for courage and God gives—
us dangers to overcome.

We ask for favors and God gives—
us opportunities.

This is the answer!

Hugh B. Brown
With Gratitude

Heavenly Father, I rejoice that this day has made me conscious of Thy presence. Thou hast led me to the end of it; Thou hast delivered me from many temptations. With gratitude, I come this hour. Let me bring cheerfulness and hope to those I meet tomorrow. In all I do or say, help me to be guided by Thy love. For Jesus' sake. Amen.

John T. Sandelin
Boy's Book of Prayers

Almighty and most merciful Father; We have erred, and strayed from thy ways like lost sheep. We have followed too much the devices and desires of our own hearts. We have offended against thy holy laws. We have left undone those things which we ought to have done; And we have done those things which we ought not to have done; And there is no health in us. But thou, O Lord, have mercy upon us, miserable offenders. Spare thou those O God, who confess their faults. Restore thou those who are penitent; According to thy promises declared unto mankind in Christ Jesus our Lord. And grant, O most merciful Father, for his sake; That we may hereafter live a godly, righteous, and sober life. To the glory of thy holy name. Amen.

The Book of Common Prayer